The Realm of No Explanation is a powerful and timely work that draws readers beyond the realm of human effort into the wonder of God's presence. With deep biblical insight and years of lived experience, Pastor Jim Raley opens the door to encounter the glory of God in a fresh and transformative way. This book will inspire and challenge every believer to step into the miracle zone where only God can receive the glory.

—REV. SAMUEL RODRIGUEZ
LEAD PASTOR, NEW SEASON CHURCH
PRESIDENT, NATIONAL HISPANIC CHRISTIAN LEADERSHIP
CONFERENCE (NHCLC)

Every once in a while a book comes along that shakes your faith in the best way possible—it pulls you out of safe, predictable Christianity and drops you into the wild, untamable mystery of God. Pastor Jim Raley has done just that with *The Realm of No Explanation*. This book isn't theory; it's truth tested in the fire of life and ministry. Pastor Raley paints a picture of a God who refuses to fit into our formulas, a God who delights in showing up where no one can take the credit. If you've ever longed for more than religion, more than explanations, and more than just another Sunday service, this book is your invitation. Step into the unexplainable. Step into revival.

—RICH WILKERSON JR.
PASTOR, VOUS CHURCH

Pastor Jim Raley's *The Realm of No Explanation* is a prophetic invitation to step beyond reason and into revelation. This book will stir your faith, awaken your hunger, and remind you that the God we serve cannot be reduced to human logic. Get ready to encounter the wonder of the unexplainable.

—BISHOP KEVIN WALLACE
LEAD PASTOR, REDEMPTION TO THE NATIONS CHURCH

In *The Realm of No Explanation*, Pastor Jim Raley shows us that God is calling His people beyond the natural and the familiar—into the miracle zone of His glory. This book is a prophetic guide that will awaken your spirit and faith to dwell where only God can be explained.

—DINO RIZZO
EXECUTIVE DIRECTOR, ASSOCIATION OF RELATED CHURCHES (ARC); ASSOCIATE PASTOR, CHURCH OF THE HIGHLANDS

Pastor Jim Raley and his entire family have a deep hunger for the presence of Jesus Christ. In *The Realm of No Explanation*, Pastor Jim speaks of the precious beauty and holiness of God's presence. He also gives a beautiful explanation of God's desire to dwell with His people, according to His own pattern. May Jesus be greatly glorified in the hearts of all who read this book.

—MICHAEL KOULIANOS
FOUNDER, JESUS IMAGE, JESUS IMAGE CHURCH, AND JESUS SCHOOL

In *The Realm of No Explanation*, Pastor Jim Raley invites readers to step beyond the natural and the familiar into the miracle dimension of God's glory. This prophetic work serves as both a guide and a call awakening the spirit and igniting faith to live in a place where only God Himself can be the explanation.

—Tony Stewart
Senior Pastor, Citylife Church
First Assistant General Overseer, Church of God

I've had the honor of serving under and walking with Apostle Jim Raley for two decades. I can say with conviction that he hasn't just preached about the glory, he's lived in it. Under his spiritual fatherhood, I've learned that when God's presence becomes my priority, I can live in a realm where heaven's reality invades my earthly calamities. *The Realm of No Explanation* isn't simply a book; it's his life scribed on paper. Every chapter carries the same anointing I've experienced under his leadership and covering. This message will stir your spirit and remind you that miracles aren't meant to be rare moments—they're the natural result of walking with a supernatural God.

—Pastor Jeremy Dunn
Kingdom Culture Church

THE REALM
OF NO
EXPLANATION

THE REALM
OF NO
EXPLANATION

JIM RALEY

CHARISMA
HOUSE

THE REALM OF NO EXPLANATION by Jim Raley
Published by Charisma House, an imprint of Charisma Media
1150 Greenwood Blvd., Lake Mary, Florida 32746

Foundation. Used by permission of Tyndale House Publishers, Carol Stream, Illinois 60188. All rights reserved.

Scripture quotations marked NLV are taken from the *New Life Version*, copyright © 1969 and 2003. Used by permission of Barbour Publishing, Inc., Uhrichsville, Ohio 44683. All rights reserved.

While the author has made every effort to provide accurate, up-to-date source information at the time of publication, statistics and other data are constantly updated. Neither the publisher nor the author assumes any responsibility for errors or for changes that occur after publication. Further, the publisher and author do not have any control over and do not assume any responsibility for third-party websites or their content.

For more resources like this, visit MyCharismaShop.com and the author's website at calvaryfl.com.

Cataloging-in-Publication Data is on file with the Library of Congress.
International Standard Book Number: 978-1-63641-573-4
E-book ISBN: 978-1-63641-574-1

1 2025
Printed in the United States of America

CONTENTS

FOREWORD

I'VE WALKED WITH the Lord long enough to know there are moments when heaven collides with earth—when the natural bows to the supernatural and you find yourself in a realm where there is no explanation except God did it. I've seen this realm break open in revival when the Spirit of God sweeps through a congregation with power, healing, and conviction that no man could manufacture. I've seen it at altars, in living rooms, and in hospital beds where the glory of God settled in and changed everything.

That's the realm Pastor Jim Raley is writing about in this book. *The Realm of No Explanation* is not theory, and it's not wishful thinking. It's an invitation to encounter the living God, who still delights in making His presence known among His people. As you read these pages, you'll be reminded that the tabernacle was never just a structure in the wilderness—it was God's prophetic blueprint of access, intimacy, and glory. Every curtain, every piece of furniture, every detail pointed to Jesus and the reality that God longs to dwell in the midst of His people.

What I love about this book is that it doesn't leave the tabernacle in the past. Pastor Raley brings it right into our present. He shows us that the same God who filled the holy of holies with unapproachable glory is the God who now fills our hearts with His Spirit. The same presence that caused priests to tremble is the presence that heals your body, restores your family, and breaks chains of bondage today.

This is not light reading. This is revelation that will stir your spirit and confront your priorities. It will call you to put God's presence at the very center of your life—not on the margins, not as an afterthought, but at the center. Because when His presence is central, everything else finds its proper place.

I believe *The Realm of No Explanation* is a timely word for the body of Christ. We are living in days of shaking. The world is desperate for something real, something powerful, something that cannot be explained away by human intellect or dismissed by human reasoning. We need the unexplainable. We need the God who parts seas, heals the sick, raises the dead, and pours out His Spirit in power. And the good news is—He has not changed.

So I encourage you: Don't just read this book. Let it read you. Let it draw you to the altar, to the laver, to the lampstand, and finally into the holy of holies where His glory dwells. Expect your faith to rise. Expect your hunger to grow. Expect to step into the realm where only God gets the glory.

Pastor Jim is not just teaching principles here; he is ushering you into an encounter. And I can promise you this—if you will lean in, if you will open your heart, you too will taste and see that the Lord is good in ways that defy all explanation.

—JOHN KILPATRICK
PASTOR, CHURCH OF HIS PRESENCE
DAPHNE, ALABAMA

MIRACLE CONNECTION

*And let them make Me a sanctuary, that
I may dwell among them.*
—EXODUS 25:8

THE HOLY OF holies was the place on earth where the manifest presence of God dwelled. It was the place where His glory came down. It was the place where mercy was offered to a people desperately in need of it. It was a place of restoration and hope. It was a place of miracles. It was the realm of no explanation.

IT'S ABOUT CONNECTION

The holy of holies was part of the wilderness tabernacle, God's dwelling place among the children of Israel as they wandered in the desert, as they entered the Promised Land, and for many years afterward until Solomon's temple was built. The tabernacle was a symbol of God's desire to connect with His people, and that connection was important. You see, God wants His people to be able to come freely into His presence. He wants them to be able to come freely into the realm of miracles, the realm of no explanation. But that starts with relationship; it starts with connection.

God wants to be present in the lives of His children. God wants to be present in *your* life. He doesn't want to be viewed as a distant God who set the universe in motion but now just sits on His throne in the heavens, uninterested in the lives of the people He created. God knows you intimately. He knows your name, the number of hairs on your head, the number of tears you have cried, your thoughts, your dreams, your heartaches and hang-ups, your fears and failures, your successes and sources of joy—every little detail about you. But the Lord God Almighty also wants to be known by you. You were created for fellowship, and God longs for you to spend time in His presence and encounter Him in a personal way—He wants you to enter the realm of no explanation.

From Genesis to Revelation, the Word of God speaks of God's agenda to stay connected with His people. Verse after verse, promise after promise, picture after picture, and event after event all witness to the fact that God wants to connect with you—from God creating man and walking with Him in the garden in the cool of the day, to God calling the children of Israel to repentance time and time again in the face of their repeated rejection of Him, to the Son of God coming to earth to be the perfect sacrifice for you and me so that we could enjoy unbroken fellowship with the Lord for eternity. And among the biblical pictures of God's desire for connection is the tabernacle. The tabernacle is about God being present in the lives of His children.

The tabernacle was the place where the children of Israel encountered God in worship as they journeyed through the wilderness en route to the Promised Land. The tabernacle is a beautiful picture of a holy God making Himself accessible and available to an unholy people. It was an invitation to believe the impossible, to have faith in the miraculous, and to experience the unexplainable. The whole tabernacle plan came straight from the heart of God. Everything you see in the tabernacle has eternal meaning. In studying the ancient wilderness tabernacle, we find striking truths and concepts that speak directly to New Testament, New Covenant believers of our day.

The tabernacle is a beautiful picture of a holy God making Himself accessible and available to an unholy people.

There's beauty and power in the tabernacle. It is full of types and shadows and prototypes that point to Jesus Christ and His finished work on the cross at Calvary. In the tabernacle that Moses constructed, you see the plan of salvation. You see the church. You see the manifestation of Jesus. You see the finished work of redemption. You see anointing. You see prayer. You see kingdom order. You see the outpouring of the Holy Spirit.

Even the materials point to Him. The ark, the brazen altar, and the table of showbread—along with other parts of the tabernacle—were all made of acacia wood. In Hebrew, the word for acacia also carries the meaning of thorn or scourge, and the word for wood carries the meaning of carpenter. Do you see it? It's all pointing to Jesus, the carpenter from Nazareth who would wear a crown of thorns and take upon Himself the scourging for our salvation.

Everything about the tabernacle points you to Jesus, points

you to His cross. And when it is in perfect order, the tabernacle is laid out in the shape of the cross. The camps of the tribes of Israel were arranged around the tabernacle, with three tribes to the north, three tribes to the south, three tribes to the east, and three tribes to the west. The three tribes to the west had the smallest population, the three tribes to the east had the largest population, and the three tribes to the north and three tribes to the south were about the same. That means even the arrangement of the camps formed the shape of the cross, with the eastern side a much longer and larger area.[1]

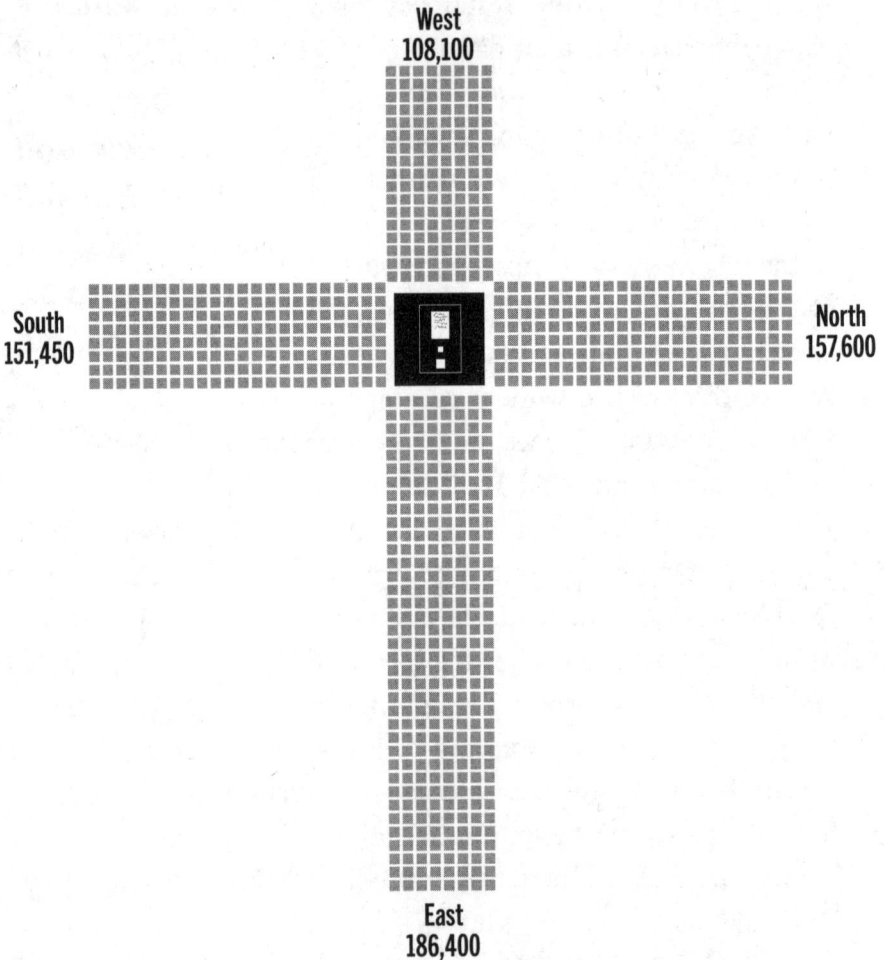

West
108,100

South
151,450

North
157,600

East
186,400

Even the layouts of the tabernacle itself and the camps surrounding it point to Jesus and the sacrifice He made so you could have unbroken fellowship with Him. And I don't know about you, but I think we are living in a time when the generations need Jesus and fellowship with Him more than ever before.

When you study the tabernacle, you can see that God was serious about His presence. The tabernacle was all about connecting with God. The tabernacle was all about God saying to His people, "I want to be in your world." God was so serious about the tabernacle that while only two chapters of the Bible are dedicated to the explanation of creation, there are over fifty chapters in the Bible dedicated to explaining the preparation, building, and function of the tabernacle and what it means to go after the presence of God. God wants you to spend time in His presence. He wants to connect with you!

BUILD YOUR LIFE

When the children of Israel were journeying through the desert, the very first thing they did when they stopped to camp, before they even set their own tents up, was put up the Tent of Dwelling, or the tabernacle. Putting up the wilderness tabernacle was their first priority. It was the place of dwelling, the place of encounter, the place of forgiveness, the place of hope, the place of miracles, and it always came first.

Next, all twelve tribes camped roundabout the tabernacle. The tribes of Dan, Asher, and Naphtali were to the north; the tribes of Reuben, Simeon, and Gad were to the south; the tribes of Ephraim, Manasseh, and Benjamin were to the west; and the tribes of Judah, Issachar, and Zebulun were to the east. Everybody put up their tents facing toward the tabernacle, toward the presence of God. They put the Lord first. The presence of God was central to the camp, and it was a picture of the way the presence of God should be central to our lives.

We need to put the Lord first in our lives. We must build our lives around His presence. We can't just squeeze God in somewhere on our lists; He is first, or He is nothing. I want you to understand that if we want to have any hope and any help in our lives, we've got to make God's presence in our lives our priority. God has to be first. If we want to experience the realm of no explanation, we need to put the Lord at the center of our lives.

We must build our lives around His presence. We can't just squeeze God in somewhere on our lists; He is first, or He is nothing.

We live in a generation that thinks we can just fit God in wherever we want Him, that we can give God the leftovers. We don't need to give God what's left; we need to give Him what's right, and what's right is what's first. You see, God is preeminent. That means He is of paramount importance. He always has been, and He always will be. There is none greater than the Lord. He reigns supreme. He is number one. Nothing comes before Him. God said, "I don't fit on your list. You can't put Me on your to-do list and make Me number three, four, or five." He said, "I'm number one or nothing."

The Bible says, "But seek first the kingdom of God and His righteousness, and all these things shall be added to you" (Matt. 6:33). Putting God first is even inherent in one of the names of the tabernacle. The wilderness tabernacle is also called the Tent of Meeting. In the Hebrew it is called the ʾōhel *môēḏ*. The first word, *'ōhel*, means tent, tabernacle, home, or dwelling place.[2] The second word, môēd, means an appointment, place of meeting, appointed place, or appointed time.[3]

So the tabernacle is the Tent of the Appointed Time. It isn't the Tent of When You Get Around to It, or the Tent of When You Have Nothing Better to Do, or the Tent of After You Do One or Two Other Things First. It is the place where you have an all-important appointment to spend time with the Lord. It is the place where you prioritize being in the presence of the One who created you, who knows you by name, who considers you priceless, who accepts you, who loves you, who forgives you, and who delights in spending time with you. It is the place where you connect with God, knowing that all those other things, everything you need, will be added to you when you seek Him first.

We live in a generation that is so mesmerized with things. We're so consumed with things. We think that if we could just have more things, we would be happier, healthier, freer, and more [fill in the blank]. But I'm telling you, at the end of the day, things cannot redeem you. Things cannot make you truly happy. Things cannot heal you. Things cannot help you. Things cannot set you free. But there is a name that is high above every other name! And that name is high above every other thing too. You need to understand that.

> The eyes of your understanding being enlightened; that you may know what is the hope of His calling, what are the riches of the glory of His inheritance in the saints, and what is the exceeding greatness of His power toward us who believe, according to the working of His mighty power which He worked in Christ when He raised Him from the dead and seated Him at His

right hand in the heavenly places, far above all princi-
pality and power and might and dominion, and every
name that is named, not only in this age but also in that
which is to come.

—EPHESIANS 1:18–21

Everything you need is found in Jesus. Jesus is the goal. Jesus
is the pursuit. Jesus is the priority. And let me tell you, when
you make Jesus your priority, you are going to experience things
beyond what you could ask or imagine. You are going to experience the supernatural, the miraculous, the unexplainable.

Some people have asked me, "Apostle Raley, what's the
secret sauce of Calvary? What has enriched the ministry
through the years?" I'll tell you exactly what our secret
sauce has been: We made God's presence our number one
priority—not buildings, not programs, not personalities, but
the presence of God. Because when it's all said and done, a
man can't deliver you, a building can't save you, and a pro-
gram can't set you free. But if you can get in the presence
of the Lord, everything changes. For "in [His] presence is
fullness of joy" (Ps. 16:11). The Lord said, "My Presence will
go with you, and I will give you rest" (Exod. 33:14). The
Word also says that "times of refreshing may come from the
presence of the Lord" (Acts 3:19). And, "where the Spirit of
the Lord is, there is freedom" (2 Cor. 3:17, ESV). So I would
admonish you as a father in the Lord to build your life
around the presence of God.

Now, right in front of the entrance into God's presence, as
you began this journey into the tabernacle, there were three
tribes camped in front: the tribe of Issachar, the tribe of
Zebulun, and the tribe of Judah. These were all very powerful

tribes. Judah was the largest tribe, and Issachar and Zebulun were among the largest too. You had to come through these camps if you were going to approach the entrance into God's presence.

We know that everything means something as it relates to the tabernacle. Even the names of these three tribes are significant because of their meanings. Issachar means a reward is coming.[4] Zebulun means exalted and comes from a word meaning either dwell or a gift.[5] Judah's name means praise.[6]

I'll say it again: Issachar's name means a reward is coming. Some of you have made God's presence your priority, and the devil is saying, "I'm going to defeat you." But I have come to testify and tell you that a reward is coming, and if you'll keep passionately pursuing the presence of God, God will shift your situation and turn it around.

Zebulun's name means dwell or gift, and then Judah, of course, means praise. You need to be dwelling in praise. You can't underestimate the power of praise. You can't underestimate the necessity of praising the Lord, of knowing what it is to praise God. Praise is necessary. Praise is not just a ritual we go through or a few songs we sing on Sunday morning. Praise has to be a lifestyle. You have to dwell in praise.

I'm tired of hearing people say, "I don't praise God because I'm too deep. I don't clap because I'm too deep. I don't lift my hands or open my mouth because I'm too deep." The reality of it all is that deep people praise God. When you open your mouth and praise God, things shift. The truth is you can pray and still be heavy, you can give and still be heavy, and you can read your Bible and still be heavy. But when you put on a garment of praise, you take off the spirit of heaviness.

The prophet Isaiah foretold that Jesus would be sent "to

heal the brokenhearted, to proclaim liberty to the captives, and the opening of the prison to those who are bound; to proclaim the acceptable year of the LORD, and the day of vengeance of our God; to comfort all who mourn, to console those who mourn in Zion, to give them beauty for ashes, the oil of joy for mourning, the garment of praise for the spirit of heaviness" (Isa. 61:1–3). When you are wearing the garment of praise, all that heaviness has to break off. There are some things that won't happen until you praise the Lord.

The tribe of Judah was the largest tribe, and it was very powerful. Judah was the tribe that led the way through the desert. Anytime the Israelites were walking through the desert, through the wilderness, Judah was out front. Judah was leading—in the hard times, in the lean times, in the struggling times. The reality is this—you need to keep your praise out front, leading the way. Praise in your hard times. Praise in your sick times. Praise in the storms, the fires, and the floods. Praise in the pandemic. Praise when you feel like crying. You open your mouth and say, "I will bless the LORD at all times; His praise shall continually be in my mouth" (Ps. 34:1).

Judah also led the Israelites in battle. Anytime they were going to fight the Hivites, the Hittites, the Amalekites, the Amorites, the Canaanites, the Perizzites, the Girgashites, or the Jebusites, praise led the way into battle. We all have -ites to fight. Some of you have been dealing with the crazy-childrenites, the bad-bossites, the nasty-neighborites, or even the demon-possessed-husbandites.

Second Chronicles tells of a time when God's children were facing a battle with an overwhelming enemy:

Then the Spirit of the LORD came upon Jahaziel the son of Zechariah....And he said, "Listen, all you of Judah and you inhabitants of Jerusalem, and you, King Jehoshaphat! Thus says the LORD to you: 'Do not be afraid nor dismayed because of this great multitude, for the battle is not yours, but God's....You will not need to fight in this battle. Position yourselves, stand still and see the salvation of the LORD, who is with you, O Judah and Jerusalem!' Do not fear or be dismayed; tomorrow go out against them, for the LORD is with you."

And Jehoshaphat bowed his head with his face to the ground, and all Judah and the inhabitants of Jerusalem bowed before the LORD, worshiping the LORD. Then the Levites of the children of the Kohathites and of the children of the Korahites stood up to praise the LORD God of Israel with voices loud and high....

And when [Jehoshaphat] had consulted with the people, he appointed those who should sing to the LORD, and who should praise the beauty of holiness, as they went out before the army and were saying: "Praise the LORD, for His mercy endures forever."

Now when they began to sing and to praise, the LORD set ambushes against the people of Ammon, Moab, and Mount Seir, who had come against Judah; and they were defeated. For the people of Ammon and Moab stood up against the inhabitants of Mount Seir to utterly kill and destroy them. And when they had made an end of the inhabitants of Seir, they helped to destroy one another. So when Judah came to a place overlooking the wilderness, they looked toward the multitude; and there were their dead bodies, fallen on the earth. No one had escaped.

—2 CHRONICLES 20:14–15, 17–19, 21–24

The children of Israel trusted in God for their victory, and they gave God praise for the victory before they even fought the battle. Their victory came from the realm of no explanation. The Israelites didn't even have to shoot a single arrow, throw a single spear, or lift a single sword. They didn't have to lift a finger, other than to clap their hands, beat their drums, shake their tambourines, and raise their hands to the Lord who fought their battles. And that is the key: You need to praise God even when you're facing what seems like a hopeless situation.

Let Satan know that the battle is already won. There is a fight, but it's a fixed fight.

You may be facing an overwhelming enemy, overwhelming odds, or overwhelming obstacles, but the battle belongs to the Lord. Anybody can praise the Lord when all their children are saved. Anybody can praise the Lord when they have money in their pockets. Anybody can praise when they have just what they want. But when all hell is breaking loose, when there's a pandemic and people are wearing masks, when everything that can go wrong is going wrong, when the enemy seems to be attacking you from every side, it's time to rise up and say, "I will give God praise." You're letting Satan know that the battle is already won. There is a fight, but it's a fixed fight. You have already won because if God is for you, who can be against you?

Let's tie it all together. You have Zebulun, meaning gift and dwell. You have Issachar, meaning a reward is coming. You have Judah, meaning praise. Here's what I think it means: When you dwell in praise, gifts and rewards are coming. You're walking right into God's presence. Breakthrough is coming. Healing is coming. Mercy is coming. Joy is coming. Redemption is coming. Power is coming. God is releasing miracles. Hell doesn't want you to know it, but your praise can bring rewards. It can bring gifts. It can bring healing. It can usher you into the realm of miracles, the realm of no explanation.

MIRACLE TIME

God wants His presence to be a reality in the lives of His people. Again, God doesn't want to be viewed as a distant God sitting on His throne far away in the heavens and disconnected from the lives of those He loves. So God said, "I'm going to do what it takes to make My presence real for My people." Way back in Old Testament times, the heavenly Father desired fellowship with His people. He desired it then, and He desires it right now. I don't know about you, but I am so glad God desires to fellowship with us!

The tabernacle was all about God being present in the lives of His children, and it was built according to certain specs and certain plans. God said, "This is how you're going to do it." God was very specific and detailed about the process. Nothing was left to chance. God said, "If you're going to connect with Me, you connect with Me on My terms. You connect with Me My way, not your way." We connect with God on His terms, not our terms.

Every single detail of the tabernacle had a plan, a purpose. It was God painting a picture of how He wants to connect with us and be present in our lives. It was God showing us His power, His glory. It was God proving that there is nothing too hard for Him. It was God saying, "You may not be able to explain it, but I can. There is nothing impossible for Me!"

Check this out: The tabernacle has three sections—the outer court, the inner court, and the holy of holies. Everything that was done in the outer court was done in natural light. It was outside the tent. The outer court represents the flesh realm. It represents the realm of the senses, where we have to see something, touch it, smell it, taste it, or hear it, or we don't experience it. Unfortunately, much of the church lives in the flesh realm, not realizing that we serve a God who is supernatural, that He confounds the laws of nature, and that He does things that we call miracles.

The outer court is the realm of things that are easily explainable. Now, just because something is easily explainable doesn't mean God isn't behind it. After all, He created the world and everything in it. He made things to function the way they do. So, for example, if you get a cut on your finger, it will eventually heal because that is how God made your body to work. It is easily explainable. Yet God wants you to move past the outer court, the realm of the easily explainable.

While everything that was done in the outer court was done in natural light, you then moved to the inner court, which was lit by the golden candlestick, or the golden lampstand. It weighed one hundred pounds and was in three separate pieces, with the number three representing the Trinity. The golden lampstand had seven lamps representing the church. The lamps were fueled by oil, and if there was no oil, there was no light. The lamps were nothing without the oil, and the church is also nothing without the oil. We're nothing without the anointing of the Holy Spirit. But when the lamps were filled with oil and then lit, they provided light for the inner court.

Everything that was done in the inner court was done by candlelight. The priest would go by the altar and wash himself at the laver in the outer court, and then he would progress into the inner court, with the table of showbread and the altar of incense, lit by the golden lampstand. Even though entering the inner court represented progress, or promotion to another dimension, there was still a dependency on the natural realm because the priest still needed somebody to bring him bread for the table and oil for the lamp. The inner court is the realm where you are still depending on a man.

God is going to bring you into the realm where there is no explanation for what is going on.

Some of you are in a season of life where you're still depending on a man. You've been counting on men to bring you through and men to give you a miracle. But I'm telling you, God is about to usher His church and His people into a new realm—a realm where your breakthrough isn't going to come because a man brought it to you, or a man provided it, or a man made it happen. God doesn't want you to stop in the outer court, the realm of the easily explainable, the realm of the flesh. He doesn't want you to stop in the inner court, where you are depending on someone else for your miracle. God wants you to go all the way in, to the holy of holies. He wants you to enter the realm of no explanation.

God is going to bring you into the realm where there is no explanation for what is going on. You see, there was natural light in the outer court, and there was candlelight in the inner court, but the glory of the Lord was the light in the holy of holies, the most holy place. It was the location of the manifest presence of God. There wasn't a natural or explainable source of light in the holy of holies; it was lit by a supernatural light source, the glory of the Lord.

I testify that I'm ready to see the glory of the Lord working miracles in my life. I testify that the Lord saved my family and turned my situation around, and it can't be explained apart from the supernatural. So all I can say is, "Look what the Lord has done!" This realm defies logic. God had to do it. The miracle-working power of God was responsible. This is the realm where you say, "I don't know how I was healed, or how I survived, or how that happened, but I left my natural world and got into His world of glory." The holy of holies is the realm of the supernatural, the unexplainable. It is the realm of no explanation. It is the realm of miracles. And that is where we want to be.

Everything about the tabernacle was specific. Everything about the tabernacle pointed us toward something else. It let us know that there was more going on. It let us know that we don't have to be limited to the realm of the natural and easily explainable or the realm where we are still dependent upon a man for our miracles.

I want to let you know today that no matter what you're facing, no matter what you feel like you're up against—maybe you've had a hard day, a hard week, a hard month, or even a hard year—there's more going on than you realize. The Lord is on your side. The Lord is inviting you to have access to the holy of holies, the realm of miracle connection, the realm of no explanation. Hallelujah!

And as we take this journey together, I want to walk with you in a very real way. Throughout this book, at the ends of several chapters I have included QR codes like the following one. Each will take you to a video of me preaching about or praying through different parts of the tabernacle. I encourage you to scan them as you read so you can encounter these truths not only with your mind but also in the Spirit—and go even deeper into the revelation of God's presence.

JimRaleyBooks.com/resources

Now let's begin the journey through the tabernacle.

Chapter 1

THE GATE: APPROACH WITH PRAISE

Enter into His gates with thanksgiving, and into His courts with praise. Be thankful to Him, and bless His name.
—PSALM 100:4

EVERYTHING STARTS WITH entering into the presence of the Lord. You have to come through the gate. If you want to get to the realm of no explanation, you can't approach the Lord your own way. God said, "You'll come My way, or you won't come at all." The Bible says, "Enter into His gates with thanksgiving, and into His courts with praise" (Ps. 100:4).

The people of Israel would approach the gate on the eastern side of the tabernacle, walking through the camps of Judah, Issachar, and Zebulun, the three tribes that were encamped under the standard of Judah, the standard of praise. As the people came through the gates, they would begin to magnify the Lord. They would begin to thank Him and praise Him for all His marvelous works. They would be thankful to Him, and they would bless His name.

Hangings of fine woven linen made a fence all the way around the tabernacle. The hangings on the north and south sides were one hundred cubits, or about 150 feet, in length, and they were hung on twenty pillars on each side. The west side of the tabernacle had hangings that were fifty cubits, or about seventy-five feet, in length, hung on ten pillars. On either side of the gate on the east side of the tabernacle, the hangings were fifteen cubits, or about twenty-two feet, in length, with three pillars for each one.

The gate itself was actually twenty cubits, or about thirty feet, wide. But the gate looked different from the rest of the hangings that made up the fence around the tabernacle. While most of the hangings were plain white, fine woven linen, the gate had a screen or curtain "woven of blue, purple, and scarlet thread, and fine woven linen, made by a weaver" (Exod. 27:16). You knew it was the gate because of the colors— blue, scarlet, and purple—that set it apart.

THE ONLY WAY

The gate was different from everything else, and it was the only way in. There wasn't a side door. There wasn't a back door. You couldn't climb over the fence, and you couldn't crawl under the fence. Jesus said you would be the same as a thief and a robber if you tried to come into God's presence any way other than the door:

> Most assuredly, I say to you, he who does not enter the sheepfold by the door, but climbs up some other way, the same is a thief and a robber.
>
> —JOHN 10:1

Jesus also said, "I am the way, the truth, and the life. No one comes to the Father except through Me" (John 14:6). He said, "Most assuredly, I say to you, I am the door of the sheep....I am the door. If anyone enters by Me, he will be saved, and will go in and out and find pasture" (John 10:7, 9). Just as there was only one way into the presence of God in the wilderness tabernacle—the gate of blue, scarlet, and purple—there is only one way into the presence of God now. Jesus is the gate. Jesus is the door.

Jesus didn't say He was *a* way, *a* truth, and *a* life. Jesus didn't say He was *a* door. Jesus is *the* way. Jesus is *the* truth. Jesus is *the* life. Jesus is *the* door. There is none other. No one comes to the Father, to the presence of the Lord God Almighty, Maker of heaven and earth, except through Jesus Christ, and Him alone. Acts 4:12 says, "Nor is there salvation in any other, for there is no other name under heaven given among men by which we must be saved." There is no other name. There is no other way. It's Jesus all the way.

Just as there was only one way into the presence of God in the wilderness tabernacle, there is only one way into the presence of God now: Jesus.

Where are the preachers in America who will rise up again and say, "Jesus is the answer"? That doesn't mean we're warring with anybody else. That doesn't mean we hate those of another religion. But I am telling you this: I will not give up the name of Jesus. He is my salvation. He is my strength. I believe in the mighty name of Jesus, and He is my door, so I can't help but open my mouth and give Him a mighty praise.

The door was different from everything else. It looked like nothing else. And don't you know Jesus is different from everything else? If you go to Buddha's tomb, he's still there. The tomb is occupied. If you go to Krishna's tomb, you will find it is occupied. If you go to Muhammad's tomb, it's occupied. But when you go to the tomb of Jesus, it is different. It is not occupied. We serve a risen Savior, and He's in the world today. That's what makes Jesus different. He conquered death and hell and the grave.

> Death is swallowed up in victory. O Death, where is your sting? O Hades, where is your victory?
> —1 CORINTHIANS 15:54–55

Now, I know this is not popular teaching, and I know a lot of people can't handle it nowadays because we've become too politically correct and so ecumenical in our philosophy. But I'm here to let you know that there is still only one way to enter into the presence of God. There is only one way into redemption. There is only one way to salvation. Buddha can't save you. Allah can't redeem you. Krishna can't turn your life around. There is a door into the presence of God, and that door is Jesus Christ. And that door is for everyone, for the Word says:

> For God so loved the world that He gave His only begotten Son, that *whoever* believes in Him should not perish but have everlasting life.
> —JOHN 3:16, EMPHASIS ADDED

> And it shall come to pass that *whoever* calls on the name
> of the Lord shall be saved.
> —Acts 2:21, emphasis added

As I mentioned, the door was thirty feet wide. Who in the world ever heard of a thirty-foot-wide door? That's extra wide. That's a *whosoever-will-come* door. You needed an extra-wide door. I needed an extra-wide door. If God had not made that door extra wide, we would have never made it in with all the junk in our trunk. But hallelujah, the Lord God made a door so wide that it doesn't matter what you've dealt with.

It doesn't matter how you've fallen. It doesn't matter what sin has done to you. It doesn't matter about that addiction. It doesn't matter about that sexual confusion. It doesn't matter about those drugs. It doesn't matter about that mouth. It doesn't matter about that divorce. It doesn't matter about that abortion. It doesn't matter about your past. Those things have no power over you because there is an extra-wide door that says, "Whosoever will come, come on in!"

The enemy is trying to keep you captive. The enemy is trying to keep you in bondage. But I'm telling you in the mighty name of Jesus that you're headed somewhere. That's the beauty of walking with the Lord; He's always taking you somewhere. Hallelujah. You're always going to another level. Aren't you glad for the door?

You Need to Know the Password

These days you need a password for just about everything. Those apps on your phone—from mobile banking and money apps to social media and shopping apps to apps that control your thermostat and your washing machine—all need a password. You can't even order chicken wings or a cheese-burger on a restaurant app without a password. We all have dozens and dozens of passwords. In fact, most of us have so many passwords that it is impossible to remember them all. I'm pretty sure I'm not the only one who has to click on "Forgot Your Password?" on a regular basis.

The gate to the tabernacle also has a password. It's not complicated or hard to remember. The password is simply this: "Thank You!" *The Message* paraphrase of the Bible writes Psalm 100:4 this way:

Enter with the password: "Thank you!"

The gate is even programmed to accept multiple variations of the same password. The way you enter the gate of the tabernacle is with thanksgiving. It doesn't matter how you phrase your thanks to the Redeemer, the Healer, the Savior, the King of kings, the Lord God Most High, the Maker of heaven and earth. You just need to enter the gate with a thankful heart, whatever that looks like and however you want to express it.

We all have plenty of things to be thankful for. The people of God need to be a thankful people. We can be thankful for the material blessings we have, like food in our bellies and roofs over our heads. We can be thankful for our families and our friends. But there is so much more to be thankful for beyond those things.

We need to be thankful for God's goodness and mercy.

Oh, give thanks to the LORD, for He is good! For His mercy endures forever.

—1 CHRONICLES 16:34

We need to be thankful for the victory we have in Christ.

> But thanks be to God, who gives us the victory through
> our Lord Jesus Christ.
> —1 Corinthians 15:57

We need to be thankful for the Word of God, the Holy Spirit at work in our lives, grace, redemption, forgiveness, access to the throne room of heaven, the love of God poured out in our hearts, the body of Jesus that was broken for us, the blood of Jesus that was shed for us... The list goes on and on. There is always something to be thankful for, so we can enter the gate "giving thanks always for all things to God the Father in the name of our Lord Jesus Christ" (Eph. 5:20). So while you do need a password to enter the gate, it is not a hard one. Just tell the Lord, "Thank You!"

PRAISE IN THE WILDERNESS

The door of the tabernacle wasn't made of wood or metal, and it didn't swing open like the doors we typically picture in our minds. The door was made of cloth, so it was rolled up. The priest would come in the door by bowing down. He would slide underneath that cloth and come into the presence of God. Psalm 95:6 says, "Oh come, let us worship and bow down." By bowing down before the Lord as he entered the tabernacle, the priest was saying, "I can't heal myself. I can't deliver myself. I can't make a way for myself. I can't save my children. I can't provide for tomorrow. So I'm going to bow down. I'm going to acknowledge that there is a power greater than my power and there is a name that is greater than my name." Hallelujah!

While the tabernacle was built as a house for the presence of God on earth, there is another way you can build a house

YOU ARE A GOOD ENGINE

for the Lord in your life. You made it through the door. You got in. So it's time to praise the Lord and build Him a house with your praise. Psalm 22:3 says, "But You are holy, O You who inhabits the praises of Israel" (MEV). That means the Holy One of Israel lives in your praise. He dwells there. When you praise the Lord, you are building Him a house.

The tabernacle is all about God wanting to be connected to His people, and the way you stay connected with Him is through your praise!

I don't believe anything seals the deal in your life for victory, breakthrough, and purpose the way your willingness and ability to give God praise does. When you praise the Lord, you are declaring that your confidence is not in your situation, your abilities, your works, your connections, your possessions, your friends, or anything else. Your praise is a declaration that all you have you only have because of the goodness of God, and every victory to come hinges on staying connected to His presence. We know that the tabernacle is all about God wanting to be connected to His people, and the way you stay connected with Him is through your praise!

There are many Hebrew words for *praise*. Each word has a different meaning, a different way of praising God, a different concept. And each concept, when put into practice, produces a divine disruption to the devil's schemes. Nothing messes up the plans and schemes of the enemy like when you learn how to praise God in every situation, especially when you are in the wilderness. When you give God all the glory and praise no matter what your circumstances are, you attract His presence. And when you attract the presence of God, the impossible becomes possible. The Lord shows up, and things begin to shift. The world may look at you and say you are hopeless and helpless, but praise shifts your focus off your situation and onto God. And you know that "with God all things are possible" (Matt. 19:26).

David wrote Psalm 63 in the wilderness:

> O God, You are my God; early will I seek You; my soul thirsts for You; my flesh longs for You in a dry and thirsty land where there is no water. So I have looked for You in the sanctuary, to see Your power and Your glory. Because Your lovingkindness is better than life, my lips shall praise You. Thus I will bless You while I live; I will lift up my hands in Your name. My soul shall be satisfied as with marrow and fatness, and my mouth shall praise You with joyful lips. When I remember You on my bed, I meditate on You in the night watches. Because You have been my help, therefore in the shadow of Your wings I will rejoice.
>
> —PSALM 63:1–7

When David wrote this psalm, where he was and who he was didn't seem to be in harmony; they were in conflict. He was anointed to be king, but he was out in the wilderness. Life was not making sense. Instead of a crown, he had a cave. Instead of living like royalty, he was on the run. Have you ever been there? Have you even been in the wilderness, where your circumstances were not lining up with what you know about who you are? What do you do when you know your call is greater, but you seem to be stuck in the wilderness? What do you do when your potential does not line up with where you are in life?

You praise the Lord.

David prayed, "O God, You are my God" (Ps. 63:1). He knew that God hadn't changed just because he was in a wilderness season. Your season doesn't change the fact that God can do exceedingly abundantly above all that you could ask or imagine (Eph. 3:20). Your season doesn't change the fact that God can move in a way that has no explanation.

The children of Israel were in the wilderness too. The tabernacle wasn't in the city. It wasn't in a nice suburb. It wasn't beachside. It was the wilderness tabernacle. Just because you are in the wilderness doesn't mean you can't praise the Lord.

Let's be honest—sometimes life stinks. But David said, "Because Your lovingkindness is better than life, my lips shall praise You" (Ps. 63:3). David understood the truth: Sometimes life does stink, but God's loving-kindness is better than life. Sometimes you go through seasons you don't like, but God is still good. So David said, "My lips shall praise You." He gave his mouth a command. He had a reason to praise, and he wasn't going to let anyone or anything stop him.

The word *because* means to have a cause and a reason. Because God is good, you have a reason to praise. Because He healed you, delivered you, saved you, you have a cause and a reason to praise. So when someone asks you, "Why do you shout?" you just say, "Because."

"Why do you clap your hands?"

"Because."

"Why are you still giving God glory?"

"Because."

"Why do you still say your children are going to get saved?"

"Because."

"Why are you still believing for a miracle?"

"Because."

David's strategy for victory in the wilderness was praise, and he knew he had a reason and a cause to praise. The word David used for praise in verse 3 is *šābaḥ*, or *shabach*. It means to announce, to pronounce, to keep in, and to remain in praise.[1] When you praise the Lord, when you shabach, you are making an announcement that God is able, that He is worthy. But beyond that, you are not going to just start praising Him; you are going to keep praising Him. You are going to remain in praise. God has been good, God is good, and God will be good. God made a way before, He is making a way right now, and He will make a way again. And because of that, you need to keep praising Him.

You're not dangerous to the enemy when you just praise the Lord for a few minutes on Sunday morning, but hell panics when you get in praise and stay there. When your children are acting crazy, stay in praise. When your money is funny, stay in praise. When people are talking bad about you, stay in praise. When you are frustrated, stay in praise. When you get a bad doctor's report, stay in praise. When you don't get the promotion, stay in praise. When your husband or your wife is acting weird, stay in praise. When the storms of life are raging, stay in praise. Wilderness times don't last always, but from the rising of the sun to the going down of the same the name of the Lord is worthy to be praised (Ps. 113:3).

I think shabach is a joy-releasing praise. David wrote, "When I remember You on my bed, I meditate on You in the night watches" (Ps. 63:6). That means even in the dark, even in the night seasons, even when you can't see what's ahead, you praise God. You remember Him because He has remembered you. That word *remember* is made of two parts: *re-*, meaning to do again, and *member*, meaning to put together. Remember God because He remembers you. Remember all the times God put you back together when you were broken, when you were struggling, when you were torn apart. Open your mouth and give God a joy-releasing shabach praise, because if He remembered you before, He will remember you again. God's not done with you, precious. He will remember you.

The other word David used for praise in Psalm 63 is *hālal*: "My mouth shall praise You with joyful lips" (v. 5). Hālal means to praise, to celebrate, to make a show of, and to boast.[2] It means to brag on God. That means you don't let your pride get in the way and get a big head when God chooses to bless you. Instead, you choose to praise Him and give Him all the glory. You boast in the fact that He made a way where there was no way. You boast in the miracle mercy He showed you. You boast in the goodness of God. You boast in the things He did that have no explanation.

Hālal is also a crazy praise. It means to go mad, to act a little bit crazy, and to even be clamorously foolish.[3] This means that even though you are in the wilderness and your circumstances don't seem to give you a reason to praise, you praise God anyway. It's praising when things don't make sense, when things are hard to understand. My children are acting crazy, but I'm still praising Him. I've got no money, but I'm still praising Him. Life is rough, but I'm still praising Him. My job is frustrating, but I'm still praising Him. My marriage is struggling, but I'm still praising Him. I'm lonely, but I'm still praising Him.

When you give God a hālal praise, the world is going to look at you and say, "You have lost your mind!" And you just say, "Yes, I have. I have lost my natural mind, and I'm depending on the Lord, who is on my side." When you know the truth of who God is and the truth of His plans for your life, you can give Him a crazy praise. You know He can do exceedingly abundantly above all that you could ask or imagine, so you can give Him a crazy praise. You know He is working all things together for your good, so you can give Him a crazy praise. You know that you are more than a conqueror in Him, so you can give Him a crazy praise. Even in the wilderness, give the Lord a crazy praise!

I think hālal is a confidence-releasing praise. When you boast in God, you are instilling confidence in yourself because you know you aren't the one who needs to fight the battle. The battle belongs to the Lord. Hālal is where we get the word *hallelujah*, which means hālal to Yah, or the Lord. Each and every time you shout "Hallelujah!" you are boasting in God. You are saying, "Lord, You are the Healer! You are the Provider! You are the Deliverer! You are the Waymaker!" And because you know God has done it before, you know He can do it again, which is why confidence is released every time you shout "Hallelujah." So shout it out: Hallelujah!

NAIL IT DOWN!

Psalm 47 is one of my favorite chapters in the whole Bible:

> Oh, clap your hands, all you peoples! Shout to God with the voice of triumph! For the LORD Most High is awesome; He is a great King over all the earth. He will subdue the peoples under us, and the nations under our feet. He will choose our inheritance for us, the excellence of Jacob whom He loves. Selah
>
> God has gone up with a shout, the LORD with the sound of a trumpet. Sing praises to God, sing praises! Sing praises to our King, sing praises! For God is the

> King of all the earth; sing praises with understanding.
> God reigns over the nations; God sits on His holy throne.
> The princes of the people have gathered together, the
> people of the God of Abraham. For the shields of the
> earth belong to God; He is greatly exalted.

This was one of about ten psalms written by the sons of
Korah. These very men were connected to the same Korah who
rebelled against Moses and ultimately against God. Because of
that, the ground opened up and swallowed Korah and everyone
else involved in the rebellion. But it seems that some of Korah's
descendants survived and separated themselves from the folly
and foolishness of Korah. These descendants of Korah became
soldiers in David's army as well as doorkeepers and worship-
leading psalmists in the house of the Lord.

Instead of following in the way of rebellion, these descendants
of Korah separated themselves from rebellion, and because
they did, God blessed them. They knew all about that pit that
swallowed up their ancestors, but it didn't swallow them. They
praised the Lord because they knew where they could have
been had God not reached down and showed them mercy.

You may be facing the same thing. Pits and pitfalls may
have taken out your cousins, your brothers and sisters, and
maybe even your mother and father, but you made it because
you chose to separate yourself from the rebellion in your
family. The truth is that generational issues and familiar
spirits may have tried to create destruction in your life. But
like the sons of Korah, what got the others is not going to
get you, because you have separated yourself and set yourself
apart for the glory of God.

No generational curse or familiar spirit is going to destroy you, because you have been saved, sanctified, redeemed, and delivered by the blood of the Lamb! You are the recipient of miracle mercy! Why not stop right now and praise God that in the mighty name of Jesus every generational curse is broken off you, your children, and your children's children! You will walk in the blessing of the Lord because those issues are broken off in the name of Jesus!

Those same men who knew they should be in a pit but were instead doorkeepers in the house of the Lord, those same men who were not bound but instead were free, wrote, "Oh, clap your hands, all you peoples! Shout to God with the voice of triumph" (Ps. 47:1). Your praise is different when you know where you would have, could have, or should have been, but instead you are walking in the blessing of the Lord. You should have been bound, but you are free. You could have been lost, but you are found. You should have been depressed, but instead you are full of the joy of the Lord. The world looks at those things and sees no explanation, but you know the truth: You are walking in the blessing of the Lord, who has no problem defying explanation.

The word *clap* is a Hebrew word used for a certain type of praise to God. When you clap, you are drawing attention to something. When the sons of Korah said, "Clap your hands," they weren't trying to draw attention to themselves, their own ability, their own intellect, their own power, their own greatness. No; they knew who deserved all the glory. They were drawing attention to the power, goodness, and glory of the Lord God Almighty because He alone is worthy of all our praise. He is the One who gives us victory, who redeems us, who saves us, who heals us, who delivers us.

When you clap your hands, you are saying, "Look what God has done!" He has turned things around. He has given you breakthrough. He has given you victory. He has freed you from bondage. He has blessed you coming in and going out. He has blessed you backward, forward, and inside out. There are enemies you faced in the past that have been completely subdued, and you will not face them anymore. There are battles you fought in past seasons that you will never have to fight again. Clap your hands, all you people!

The psalm goes on to say, "Sing praises to God, sing praises! Sing praises to our King, sing praises! For God is the King of all the earth; sing praises with understanding" (Ps. 47:6–7). It says five times to sing praises. And it says to sing praises with understanding. God doesn't want you to praise Him out of ignorance or just go through the motions. Think about the goodness of God and praise Him according to His marvelous works in your life. Praise Him reflecting on the things He has done for you. Praise Him in excitement about what He is doing for you. Praise Him in anticipation of what He is about to do for you.

The word used for *praise* in verses 6 and 7 is *zāmar*. It means to play music skillfully and to sing unto the Lord.[4] Zāmar represents a prepared praise. It represents a praise that you have thought about and prepared for. It says, "I came ready. I have something to offer God." It is a praise you are carrying around in your heart, ready for the moment when the blessings of God prompt you to release it. You prepare and give God your best praise because He is worthy!

Let's go back to that word *clap* in verse 1. The Hebrew word is *tāqa*. It means to strike, to smite, or to drive a nail.[5] So when you clap your hands, it is the praise that nails things down. Some things aren't released until you praise the Lord. Some things aren't nailed down until you praise the Lord. So clap your hands! It's time to seal the deal. It's time to nail that victory down. There are battles you have already won because of the goodness of God, and praise the Lord, you won't have to fight those battles again. Clap those hands!

And don't just clap. Shout unto God with the voice of triumph! The Hebrew word for shout is *rûa*. It means breath, or to use your breath to shout unto God. It's the very same word used in the Book of Joshua when the children of Israel fought the battle of Jericho. They walked around those walls seven times. They shouted, they opened up their mouths to praise God, and those walls that were in their way came tumbling all the way down.

You may be in the wilderness. You may be struggling. You may be in the middle of some hard times. But when you approach the gate of the tabernacle, when you come into the presence of the Lord, approach with praise. You can approach with shabach, the joy-releasing praise announcing that you know God is going to remember you. You can approach with halal, the confidence-releasing, crazy praise that knows that despite what your circumstances look like, God is able to do exceedingly abundantly above all that you could ask or imagine. You can approach with zamar, the prepared praise, the praise you have ready to offer to God at a moment's notice. You can approach with rua, a shout of praise for the victory you have already received and the victory that is still to come. Or you can approach with taqa, the praise that nails it down.

Whatever way you choose to praise the Lord is fine. Just praise Him! He is worthy! His is the name above every other name! He has blessed you, called you, redeemed you, forgiven you, delivered you, healed you, chosen you, and accepted you. He alone is worthy of all praise. Amen.

PRAYER

Today, Lord Jesus, I'm going to come through the gate into Your glorious presence, and I'm going to be thankful. I'm going to glorify Your name, Jesus! I'm going to magnify You in this moment and tell You that You alone are worthy of my praise! I'm going to lift You up, Lord.

God, You said in Your Word that if I would praise You, I could enter into Your presence. So thank You for everything that You've done for me. Thank You for making a way for me where there seemed to be no way. Thank You for saving me and redeeming me and healing me.

Lord, You said in Your Word that You inhabit the praises of Your people. So today, God, I'm building Your house. If You inhabit it, then You live there. If You inhabit it, You dwell there. So Lord, I'm going to build You a house today. I'm going to offer thanksgiving to You. I'm going to thank You for what You have already done. I'm going to thank You for what You are doing. I'm going to thank You for what You are about to do. God, You are so good. Your lovingkindness is better than life. Even in the wilderness, I'm going to praise Your name!

JimRaleyBooks.com/chp1

Chapter 2

ALL ON THE ALTAR

And almost all things are by the law purged with blood;
and without shedding of blood is no remission.
—HEBREWS 9:22, KJV

RIGHT INSIDE THE gate of the wilderness tabernacle is the brazen altar. The brazen altar is where the blood flowed. The brazen altar is where the sacrifice was made. Now, we all want to get to the mercy seat because the mercy seat is where the miracles are. We all want mercy seat miracles. We all want to get to the realm of no explanation. But the reality is you can't get to mercy seat miracles unless you first come by the altar.

The brazen altar is the place where we first connect with God and where He connects with us in the redemption process. It is a place of covenant and connection. The brazen altar represents the cross of Jesus Christ. It represents the blood. I want to bring everything I have and everything I am to the altar—every hope, every dream, every struggle, every failure, every issue. I want to lay it all at the feet of Jesus. I want to put it all on the altar.

YOU'RE IN REMISSION

The priest would come in through the gate of praise with thanksgiving, and the first thing he would see was the brazen altar. This was the beginning of the process of getting to the ark, to the glory, to the place of miracles, the holy of holies. The altar was the place of sacrifice. The Lord told Moses:

> You shall make an altar of acacia wood, five cubits long and five cubits wide—the altar shall be square—and its height shall be three cubits. You shall make its horns on its four corners; its horns shall be of one piece with it. And you shall overlay it with bronze. Also you shall make its pans to receive its ashes, and its shovels and its basins and its forks and its firepans; you shall make all its utensils of bronze. You shall make a grate for it, a network of bronze; and on the network you shall make four bronze rings at its four corners. You shall put it under the rim of the altar beneath, that the network may be midway up the altar. And you shall make poles for the altar, poles of acacia wood, and overlay them with bronze. The poles shall be put in the rings, and the poles shall be on the two sides of the altar to bear it. You shall make it hollow with boards; as it was shown you on the mountain, so shall they make it.
>
> —Exodus 27:1–8

The brazen altar was the biggest piece of furniture in the entire tabernacle. It was so big—about 250 cubic feet—that all the other furniture in the tabernacle presumably could have fit inside it. Here's the thing: We often want little altars and big mercy seats. We want big miracles, but we want to bypass the altar and all it stands for. We want to build little altars and have big miracles, but the Lord is looking for people who want to be in covenant with Him, to connect with Him—and that starts at the altar.

The miracle process can't bypass the altar. The mercy seat was actually small compared to the altar. So here is what you need to know: The bigger the altar, the bigger the mercy seat. The bigger the altar, the bigger the connection. The bigger the altar, the bigger the breakthrough. The bigger the altar, the bigger the miracle. The more you trust God, the more God gives you breakthroughs.

We often want little altars and big mercy seats. We want big miracles, but we want to bypass the altar and all it stands for.

Do you need a breakthrough? You don't need a bigger bank account; you need a bigger altar. You may think you need a bigger opportunity, but you really need a bigger altar. When you build a big altar, everything else comes into line. When you build a big altar, it alters your life. It alters your circumstances. It alters your problems. It alters your family, your issues, your children, your sin. Your altar will alter you. When you spend time at the altar, everything changes. You can't spend time at the altar and leave the same way you came. Hallelujah!

The priests offered two lambs on the altar each day, according to the Lord's instructions. One was offered in the morning, and one was offered at twilight. It was the blood sacrifice. Remember, everything about the tabernacle points you to a fulfillment in the New Testament, in the New Covenant.

The brazen altar was the place where the blood flowed. The brazen altar was the place where the sacrifice gave its life. The brazen altar was where the innocent died for the guilty. The brazen altar, then, represents the cross of Jesus Christ. It's the place where we understand that there is wonder-working power in the blood of the Lamb. It's where we understand that we cannot redeem ourselves, but there is a cross, an altar, where Jesus died and shed His blood for us.

Hebrews 9:22 says, "And almost all things are by the law purged with blood; and without shedding of blood is no remission" (KJV). This is something I talk about during Communion: remission of sin. When the blood of a spotless sacrifice flows, sin is put in remission. We often use the word *remission* in connection with cancer. If you've ever dealt with cancer, it's the word you long to hear. *Remission* means something has been stopped, canceled, or restored to its former condition. If the physician says, "You're in remission," it means they've checked your entire body—your organs, your blood, your bones—and your cancer is gone.

When the blood flows, your sin is put in remission. When you are covered by the precious blood of the Lamb who takes away the sins of the world, the Great Physician is telling you, "Your sin is in remission." The Great Physician is telling you there is no sin in your body.

Once your sin is covered with the blood, the blood puts the sin in remission. That means your past is in remission. Your failure is in remission. Your compromise is in remission. All the times you have crossed the line or missed the mark are covered by the blood of Jesus. You don't have to walk around burdened by guilt and the weight of your sin because your sin is in remission. If that doesn't make you want to give the

Lord a mighty praise, I don't know what will. Praise the Lord! My sin is in remission!

Only the blood of Jesus will put your sin in remission. Denominationalism cannot put your sin in remission. Being a good person can't put your sin in remission. Being gifted or smart can't put your sin in remission. Giving an offering or doing penance or a hundred good deeds can't put your sin in remission. But the blood of Jesus Christ covers every sin that you've ever committed. When you come to the altar, your sin is in remission.

JUST AS IF I'D NEVER SINNED

When the Lord gave instructions for Passover, He told the children of Israel to have each household sacrifice a lamb and put the blood on the doorposts and lintels of their homes. In Exodus 12:13 the Lord said, "When I see the blood, I will pass over you." The word *pass* in the Hebrew is *pāsah*. It means to hop, to skip over, to leap, or to jump.[1] The Lord said He would hop, skip, leap, and jump over when He saw the blood. Not when He saw your denominational card. Not when He saw your good works. Not when He saw what you think of yourself. Not when He saw your money. He said, "When I see the blood, I will pass over you."

You've got to understand that if you've been covered by the blood, when God looks at you, He doesn't see your past. He doesn't see your failures. He doesn't even see your strengths or your weaknesses. When He looks at you, He sees the blood of Jesus. Hallelujah! It's the blood that keeps you safe. It's the blood that gives you strength. It's the blood that gives you power.

You have no idea how many times the devil looked at you and said, "I've got her now," "I'll take her family now," "I'll take his future now," "I'll take his joy now," "I'll take her peace now," or "I'll take his purpose now," but when he came at you, he saw the blood. You may have faced a lot of things, but there are also things that never got to you, things that never touched your children, things that never touched your family—all because when the devil saw the blood, the blood spoke up and said, "Back off! They belong to Jesus." The Bible says the blood of Jesus "speaks better things" (Heb. 12:24). Hallelujah! The blood is talking. The devil wants to come to your house, but the blood says, "You better back up. You can't get in. The blood covers this home."

The blood is powerful. The blood that flowed at the brazen altar is a symbol of our justification. Your sin is covered by the blood. The Bible says, "As far as the east is from the west, so far has He removed our transgressions from us" (Ps. 103:12). It doesn't say as far as the north is from the south—although that's pretty far, it's a measurable distance. The north and south poles are about 12,500 miles apart. If you start out going north, you will eventually end up going south. But if you start out going east, you can keep going and going and going, and you will never be going west. They are infinitely far apart. As far as the east is from the west—infinitely far—is how far the Lord removes your sin from you. He says, "I don't remember it anymore."

I don't know about you, but I'm thankful today to know that my sin is underneath the blood of Jesus Christ and I have been justified. *Justified* means God sees me just as if I'd never sinned. When Jesus looks at you, when God looks at you, He doesn't see that compromise, He doesn't see that abortion, He doesn't see that failure, He doesn't see that gossip, He doesn't see that lie, He doesn't see that sin, He doesn't see that anger, He doesn't see that record, He doesn't see that unforgiveness. No; when the Lord looks at you, all the Father sees is the blood of Jesus Christ. We have been justified by the blood, restored to a spotless condition, just as if we had never sinned. Praise the Lord!

ALTERED BY GRACE

Now check this out: The altar was five cubits long, five cubits wide, and three cubits tall. Five is the number of grace in the Bible. There are many examples, but let's look at a few and how they connect to the altar.

It was the fifth day of creation when God filled the waters of the earth with life. The waters were filled with "an abundance" of life, with all kinds of living creatures (Gen. 1:20). Because of the altar and because of what Jesus did, you and I are filled with living water. The Lord is "the fountain of living waters" (Jer. 2:13). Jesus said, "He who believes in Me, as the Scripture has said, out of his heart will flow rivers of living water" (John 7:38).

Jesus also told the Samaritan woman at the well, "If you knew the gift of God, and who it is who says to you, 'Give Me a drink,' you would have asked Him, and He would have given you living water....Whoever drinks of this water will thirst again, but whoever drinks of the water that I shall give him will never thirst. But the water that I shall give him will become in him a fountain of water springing up into everlasting life" (John 4:10, 13–14).

Because of Jesus' sacrifice, because of His precious blood that flowed for our justification, we can have abundant life with rivers of living water flowing into us and then out of us. That means if you are thirsty for the things of God, money can't satisfy you, prestige can't satisfy you, and going to another level in the eyes of man can't satisfy you. The thirst in you can be satisfied only by grace-filled living water. When people reject you, Jesus says, "Have a drink of My living water." When people doubt you, Jesus says, "Have a drink of My living water. I'll do for you what they can never do for you."

Here's another five connected with grace: The fifth time Noah is named in the Bible is in Genesis 6:8: "But Noah found grace in the eyes of the LORD." Do you know where you find grace? You find grace right at the altar. When you cannot find grace anywhere else, you'll find it at a blood-soaked altar, at the cross of Jesus Christ. When people say you don't deserve grace, when people say you've gone too far, when people say you've failed too much, your past is too deep, your struggle has been too much, your sin is too grievous, you need to know something. There is an altar that is five by five; it is grace coming and grace going. And grace will meet you at the altar.

The tabernacle is full of fives: five curtains coupled to each other, five bars of acacia wood for the boards on one side of the tabernacle, five pillars with five sockets of bronze, five hundred shekels of myrrh in the anointing oil, etc. The details and dimensions of the tabernacle are full of fives, and that points us to grace. The fives held the tabernacle together and held it up. And let me tell you, grace is what holds you together and holds you up. It's not your gift, it's not your ability, it's not your goodness that holds your life up and holds you together. It's grace—the unmerited, undeserved favor of a holy God.

If we got what we deserved, we wouldn't even be alive— but by the grace of God we have forgiveness, mercy, blessings, joy, peace, love, hope, freedom, and abundant life. It doesn't matter what you've done; grace is waiting for you at the altar. Grace is for everybody. You can't judge people who have fallen because grace is still at the altar. Grace may not be in some churches, but let me tell you, it's still at the altar. Grace may not be in some denominations, but it's still at the altar. And remember, the altar alters you. Grace changes you.

Romans 5:20 says, "Where sin abounded, grace abounded much more." Don't let the devil convince you that you've sinned too much or messed up too often or crossed too many lines to receive grace. God's grace is abundant. Not only that, but His grace is sufficient for you, and His strength is made perfect in weakness (2 Cor. 12:9).

If you are walking around under the weight of your sin, there is grace at the altar for you, and that grace is 100 percent free. Grace isn't cheap—

The altar alters you.

it was bought at a high price, purchased with the blood of Jesus on the cross at Calvary—but it is free for the asking. If you are carrying around a burden of sin, come to the altar. Repent, lay everything on the altar, receive the forgiveness and grace of the Lord, and walk in freedom.

There was another five in the tabernacle: The holy anointing oil is made up of five ingredients: myrrh, cinnamon, sweet-smelling cane, cassia, and olive oil. The priests were consecrated with the anointing oil so they could minister to the Lord in the tabernacle. When they approached the altar, they came with the anointing. And let me tell you, yoke-destroying, burden-lifting, grace-giving anointing is found at the altar. What you can't do in the flesh you can do once you get underneath the anointing. It will break every yoke. It will lift every burden. It will give you the grace to accomplish what you cannot accomplish on your own. Find power at the altar!

When King David was still just a shepherd boy, he faced off against a giant. And do you know what he did? He collected five smooth stones from a brook. That giant didn't stand a chance. David killed Goliath and won the victory. So while five is the number of grace, it also reminds us of the victory we have when we rely on the power of the Lord God Almighty!

Are you under attack? Are you facing giants in your life? Does the devil have you pressed down, messed up, and stressed out? You need to hear this now: There is giant-killing power found at the altar. When the devil has you under attack, come to the altar. When the enemy has your back against the wall, come to the altar. When you feel helpless or hopeless, come to the altar and you will find grace and power.

When you come to the altar, you don't leave as a victim; you leave as a victor. When you come to the altar, you don't leave overcome; you leave as an overcomer. When you come to the altar, you don't leave defeated; you leave triumphant. You may come to the altar downtrodden and downhearted, but you can walk out with your head held high, saying, "Where's the giant now? I've got grace, and I've got power. No giant is going to defeat me because the Lord's grace is sufficient for me, and there is no giant He can't take out."

DEAD OR ALIVE

We talked about the number five because two of the dimensions of the brazen altar were five cubits. But the brazen altar was also three feet high. Three is also a powerful number. Three represents unity. It represents harmony. It specifically represents the unity and harmony of the Godhead. And here is what is so powerful about the altar: Because it is a place of unity and harmony, everything that causes disunity and discord dies at the altar.

Racism dies at the altar. Sexism dies at the altar. Classism dies at the altar. All prejudices and attitudes that cause division die at the altar. Do you know why? Everyone—no matter what they look like, no matter how much money they have in the bank, no matter how they were raised, no matter who they are or how they are different—has to come to the same altar. A white man has to come to the same altar as a black man. A black man has to come to the same altar as a Hispanic man. A Hispanic man has to come to the same altar as an Asian man. Men and women have to come to the same altar. Rich, poor, and everyone in between have to come to the same altar. So don't strut around and act like you're better than others because you have more money or because you're this race or you're that race.

One problem with the church in America is that much of the church has left the altar. You can't be angry, divided, and consumed by discord and unforgiveness when you've been to the altar. We all need the blood, and we all need the altar. When we truly understand all that the altar stands for and everything Jesus sacrificed so we could connect with Him, all that mess dies. All the prejudice dies.

The number three isn't just about things that cause division dying. Yes, the altar results in dead things, but the altar also results in things coming to life! You see, three is the number of the Trinity—the Father, the Son, and the Holy Ghost. Jesus has manifested mercy at the altar. When you come to the altar, the Father cleanses you. The Holy Ghost empowers you at the altar.

You need all those things to live the abundant life Jesus

promised you. But let me go just a little bit deeper. Three is also the number of the resurrection. Jesus rose from the grave on the third day. Three is the number of dead things coming back to life. When you come to the altar, dead things come back to life. When you come to the altar, the dreams and purposes of God in your life that the devil destroyed with his lies and his schemes are going to come back to life!

When you connect with the Lord at the altar, He will breathe on your future and bring the good things you thought were dead back to life. Your hope may have died, but hope is resurrected at the altar. Your joy may have kicked the bucket, but God is going to flip that bucket right side up and fill it to overflowing at the altar. Your peace may have been six feet under for a while, but the Lord will bring it back to life at the altar. The altar is the place where the junk in your trunk dies and all the blessings of the Lord come to life. Hallelujah!

PRAYER

Jesus, I come to the altar, and I thank You that You became my sacrifice. I thank You, Lord, that You did for me what I could not do for myself. Thank You for all that You did for me on Calvary. Thank You that my sin is in remission because of the power of Your blood. Thank You that I am justified by the blood of the Lamb.

Lord, I pray that when I come to the altar, the altar will alter me. Lord, I thirst for You. Thank You for the living water. Thank You for the grace that holds me up and holds me together. Thank You that where my sin abounds, Your grace abounds much more. Lord, Your grace is sufficient for me.

Lord, forgive me for anything in my heart that causes disunity and discord; let it all die at the altar. I lay my burdens at the altar, and I choose to receive mercy. I choose to walk in freedom. Thank You, Lord, that the altar is a place where good things come back to life. I praise You for restoring my hope, my joy, and my peace at the altar. I praise You, Lord, for all Your goodness in my life.

JimRaleyBooks.com/chp2

Chapter 3

THE OFFERING

*I beseech you therefore, brethren, by the mercies of
God, that you present your bodies a living sacrifice, holy,
acceptable to God, which is your reasonable service.*
—ROMANS 12:1

THE BRAZEN ALTAR was a place of offering. It was the
place of sacrifice. We already talked about the daily offerings, the two lambs offered each day, one in the morning and
one at twilight. But there were other offerings, other sacrifices being made regularly at the tabernacle. All the offerings
made on the altar were a sweet aroma to the Lord, and they
were part of the process of getting to the holy of holies, the
realm of no explanation.

When the priest brought the sacrifices to the Lord, when
he approached the altar with the daily offering or some of
the other offerings, the sacrifice was heavy. A year-old lamb

weighs around one hundred pounds. Goats weigh quite a bit too, as do all the pieces of a bull that were part of some offerings. These sacrifices were heavy. They were difficult to lift. And remember, the altar was three cubits, or about four and a half feet tall. There would have been a lot of priests with sore backs if they had to lift the sacrifices that high all the time; they needed a way to get the offerings up to the altar.

There were no steps leading up to the altar. Instead, the altar had a ramp leading up to it. The Lord was very clear that there weren't to be any steps leading to His altar: "Nor shall you go up by steps to My altar" (Exod. 20:26). There were a couple of reasons for this. Steps leading up to an altar were associated with pagan worship of false gods. There were ramps and not steps because steps were what people climbed when they were going to worship a false god. Pagan priests actually exposed themselves while going up the steps to altars as part of their rituals. Steps pointed people toward sexual immorality and adultery.

The other reason there were ramps and not steps was given by the Lord Himself: "Nor shall you go up by steps to My altar, that your nakedness may not be exposed on it" (Exod. 20:26). While this could apply to avoiding similarities with pagan worship, it also has to do with the priest exposing his flesh. There was to be no flesh seen at the altar. Because priests wore robes, in order to walk up steps, a priest would have to hike up his robe a bit to keep from tripping and falling. But when the priest hiked up his robe, you would see his flesh. Since flesh wasn't to be seen at the altar, there was a ramp instead of steps.

Flesh dies at the altar. A true altar is a place where you get real.

Flesh dies at the altar. A true altar is a place where you get real. You don't hide anything from God, and your flesh has to die. There are people trying to get on this step or that step and go to this level or that level. But what you really need to do is bring a sacrifice to the Lord and say, "God, if there's anything in me that grieves You, if there's anything in my flesh that should not be there, let it perish now. Let me get to Your altar."

FIVE OFFERINGS

There were five different types of offerings described in the first five chapters of Leviticus, the third book of the Law: the burnt offering, the grain offering, the peace offering, the sin offering, and the trespass offering. Each of the different offerings gives us insight into the heart of God and how we can better connect with Him.

Burnt offering

The burnt offering is described in Leviticus 1. A burnt offering was a freewill offering, and it could be a bull, a sheep, a goat, a turtledove, or a pigeon. The Hebrew word for burnt *offering* is *ʿōlâ*. In addition to meaning burnt offering, it also means to ascend, to climb higher.[1]

The burnt offering was completely consumed on the altar. No parts of it were reserved for the priest. The whole thing was offered up as a sacrifice, and it produced "a sweet aroma to the Lord" (Lev. 1:9, 13, 17). The aroma of the offering rose up; it ascended before the Lord, and it pleased Him.

Here's what you need to understand and get deep down in your spirit: If you want to rise up, you have to come to the altar. You will never rise to meet the fullness of your God-given potential without the altar in your life. If you want to rise, to ascend, to climb higher, you have to come to the altar. But beyond that, if you want to rise, you need to offer all of yourself as a free-will offering to the Lord. That pleases Him; it produces a sweet-smelling aroma that rises to heaven.

It's that *all* part that trips a lot of people up. Some people think, "I'll offer the Lord this but not that," "I'll offer a few hours of my time, but that's it," or "I'll offer the Lord a lot of things as long as those things don't include my money or my family or my [fill in the blank]." But the Lord wants all of you. And when you are willing to say, "Yes, Lord! Take all of me!" you will rise in ways you never could have imagined.

Grain offering

The grain offering is described in Leviticus 2. There is some confusion about this offering because the King James Version of the Bible calls it a "meat offering" (Lev. 2:1), but there isn't any chicken or beef or anything else we typically think of as meat involved. Instead, the offering was grain—fine flour with oil and frankincense; baked unleavened cakes with oil; or roasted green heads of grain with oil and frankincense. None of the grain offerings had leaven, or yeast, in them. Leaven symbolizes sin. Offerings given to the Lord needed to be pure, so only unleavened bread was offered. A portion of the grain offering was reserved for the priests, but the rest of it was burned on the altar.

The Hebrew words translated "grain offering" or "meat offering" are *minhâ* and *qārbān*. The first word, minhâ, means a gift, donation, tribute, or sacrificial offering.[2] The second word, qārbān, means an offering, something brought close to the altar; a sacrificial gift or present.[3] So the grain offering was like a gift to the Lord. It was a tribute. *Tribute* means "something given or contributed voluntarily as due or deserved; especially a gift...showing respect, gratitude, or affection."[4] The grain offering was a way for the children of Israel to show the Lord they understood He was deserving of their thanks, their love, and their respect.

Does the Lord deserve your thanks? Offer Him a sacrifice of praise. Does He deserve your love? Lift your hands in worship in honor of His goodness. Does God deserve your respect? Come before Him with thanksgiving for His mercy, His grace, His justice, and His greatness.

Each of the grain offerings required oil. The grain, the bread, represents the Word of God. The oil represents the Holy Spirit. You need oil for the bread, and you need the Spirit for the Word. There are people who read the Bible and think it is a dry, boring book. They often don't understand what they are reading, or they just read it like they would a textbook. But oh, precious, when you have the Holy Spirit, the Word isn't dry. The Word comes alive and speaks right to your heart. The Holy Spirit opens the eyes of your understanding, and He writes His Word on the tablet of your heart.

Have you ever read a Scripture passage you have read a hundred times before, but the Spirit makes you see it in a whole new light? Have you ever had a verse jump right off the page or off your screen and change your whole way of thinking? Have you ever landed on just the right verse at just the right time to extinguish the fiery-dart lies the enemy was trying to get you to believe? That is the bread and the oil, the Word and the Spirit, working together in your life. That makes me want to give the Lord a mighty praise!

Peace offering

The peace offering is described in Leviticus 3. The Hebrew word for peace offering is *šelem*. It means a voluntary sacrifice made in thanks or a sacrifice made to confirm an alliance or friendship.[5] It comes from the root word *šālam*, which means peace, to be safe, to be complete or sound, to make amends, to finish, to reward, to be full, or to make good.[6] Šālam is also the root word of *shalom*, the Hebrew word used as a greeting or when parting that means peace, completeness, safety, welfare, health, prosperity, contentment, tranquility, and so much more.[7]

Peace offerings could be made in thanksgiving, as part of a vow, or as a voluntary offering (Lev. 7:15–16). The peace offering came from the herd or the flock. Certain parts of the sacrifice, the parts that could not be eaten according to the Law, were burned on the altar. The flesh of the sacrifice could be eaten either the same day or on the next day depending on the reason behind the sacrifice, by the person making the offering, or by whoever was involved in the alliance or friendship motivating the offering.

Peace offerings were about connection with the Lord and with others. I don't know about you, but I need to connect to the Lord, and I also need the Lord to be involved in my connections with other people. I need the Lord in my marriage. I need the Lord in my friendships. I need the Lord in my relationships with my children, my family, my neighbors, my coworkers, and everyone else.

I need the peace of God. I need the contentment, tranquility, safety, health, welfare, and completeness that only the Lord can provide. You see, if I depend on others to meet the needs in my heart and soul that only the Lord can truly meet, it affects my relationships—and not in a good way. But if I come before the Lord with people, it connects us in a way that makes it so much easier to be at peace with them, to be content in my relationships, and even to make amends when I need to.

When you come to the altar, you can lay down all the junk in your trunk that messes up your relationships. When you come to the altar, you can connect with the Lord and in turn connect with others in a way you never could before. When you come to the altar, you find peace. I don't know about you, but that sure sounds good to me. Praise the Lord!

Sin offering

The sin offering is described in Leviticus 4. The Lord said that sin offerings were for when "a person sins unintentionally against any of the commandments of the LORD in anything which ought not to be done" (Lev. 4:2). The Hebrew word for sin offering is *ḥaṭṭā'āṯ*. It means an offense or sin and its penalty or sacrifice, as well as the purification from sin.[8] The root word of hattā'āt is *ḥāṭā'*, which means to miss the mark.[9]

We all sin. We all miss the mark. Romans 3:23 says, "All have sinned and fall short of the glory of God." The word *sin* refers to those unintentional mistakes and messes we all make. Just because you didn't mean to do something or plan it ahead of time doesn't mean it isn't a sin, something that would separate you from a holy God if it weren't atoned for. So when your kids are getting on your last nerve and you react in anger, or when you tell that little lie when you get put on the spot about a mistake you made, or when you indulge in listening to that juicy gossip or harboring an impure thought, that's sin.

Before Jesus came as the perfect sacrifice for all our sin, a bull had to be offered at the tabernacle to atone for that sin.

And the Lord didn't just give instructions about individual sin; He also gave instructions about congregational sin:

> Now if the whole congregation of Israel sins uninten-
> tionally, and the thing is hidden from the eyes of the
> assembly, and they have done something against any
> of the commandments of the LORD in anything which
> should not be done, and are guilty; when the sin which
> they have committed becomes known, then the assembly
> shall offer a young bull for the sin, and bring it before
> the tabernacle of meeting.
> —LEVITICUS 4:13–14

There are times when repentance is needed on a group level. Let me tell you, there are a whole lot of people out there who were raised to think that some people are better than others because of the color of their skin, including a bunch of people in the church. But I am here to tell you that racism or prejudice of any kind is a sin. We were all made in the image of God, and we all have to come to the same altar, regardless of the color of our skin, just like we talked about in the last chapter.

If you were raised to believe that someone was inferior because of their skin color, you may not have even realized it was a sin—the reality of that sin may have been hidden from you. But if you have been guilty of that sin, now that it has been revealed to you, you need to repent.

The truth is that the body of Christ has often been guilty of the sin of prejudice, and that ought not to be. But if we repent, if we come to the altar together, if we recognize that we all have sinned and fallen short of the glory of God, there is for-giveness and grace to cover all our sin, and the healing can begin.

As the body of Christ, we are supposed to be united, not divided. We are all brothers and sisters in the family of God, no matter the color of our skin. Galatians 3:28 says, "You are all one in Christ Jesus." The externals don't matter one bit. We are one body, and we need to act like it. And if we aren't, then we have missed the mark, and we need to repent and get back on track.

The good news is that Jesus' blood covered all our sin. When He died on the cross, it was the ultimate sin offering. It wiped our slates clean. But that doesn't mean we don't need to repent, to turn from our sin and turn to God. The altar is where we do that. It is the place we go to find mercy and grace, and to have all our sins washed away. Praise the Lord!

Trespass offering

The fifth type of offering is the trespass offering, described in Leviticus 5. The Hebrew word for trespass offering is *'āšām*. It means guilt, a fault, or compensation for an offense.[10] Its root word means to be guilty, to do wrong, to commit an offense, to be incriminated, to be held guilty.[11] *Trespass* means "to enter unlawfully upon the land of another; to make an unwarranted or uninvited incursion."[12] When you are trespassing, you are crossing a line you know you aren't supposed to cross.

God's Word is full of "No Trespassing" signs. Those signs are there to protect us, to keep us from crossing lines and going to places that will harm us and harm others. But just as we all sin, we have all trespassed at one time or another. We have all crossed the line. We have all gone places we shouldn't have gone.

The good news is that there is atonement available for all our trespasses. Just like with our sin, if we come to the altar and repent, we receive forgiveness full and free. The children of Israel had to bring a sacrifice to the altar—a ewe, a lamb, a goat, two turtledoves or pigeons, or an ephah of fine flour. But for New Covenant believers like you and me, Jesus was both our sin offering and our trespass offering. His death on the cross at Calvary covered it all. Isaiah 53:10 says that Jesus made "His soul an offering for sin." The phrase *offering for sin* is the word *'āšām,* the trespass offering.

The reality is that Jesus' death on the cross covered all kinds of sin: missing-the-mark sin, crossing-the-line trespasses, rebelling-against-God transgressions, and buried-deep iniquities.

> Surely He has borne our griefs and carried our sorrows; yet we esteemed Him stricken, smitten by God, and afflicted. But He was wounded for our transgressions, He was bruised for our iniquities; the chastisement for our peace was upon Him, and by His stripes we are healed. All we like sheep have gone astray; we have turned, every one, to his own way; and the LORD has laid on Him the iniquity of us all. He was oppressed and He was afflicted, yet He opened not His mouth; He was led as a lamb to the slaughter, and as a sheep before its shearers is silent, so He opened not His mouth....For He was cut off from the land of the living; for the transgressions of My people He was stricken. And they made His grave with the wicked—but with the rich at His death, because He had done no violence, nor was any deceit

in His mouth. Yet it pleased the LORD to bruise Him; He has put Him to grief. When You make His soul an offering for sin, He shall see His seed, He shall prolong His days, and the pleasure of the LORD shall prosper in His hand. He shall see the labor of His soul, and be satisfied. By His knowledge My righteous Servant shall justify many, for He shall bear their iniquities. Therefore I will divide Him a portion with the great, and He shall divide the spoil with the strong, because He poured out His soul unto death, and He was numbered with the transgressors, and He bore the sin of many, and made intercession for the transgressors.

—ISAIAH 53:4–12

Jesus paid it all. When you come to the altar, there is no sin that can't be forgiven. When you come to the altar, there is mercy for every trespass. When you come to the altar, there is grace to cover transgressions and iniquities and everything else that might separate you from God. God made sure of it because He wants to connect with *you*. He doesn't want you separated from Him because of your sin, so He made a way. Because He is holy, He can't have the unholy in His presence, and that is why He sent Jesus. Because of His sacrifice, "you, who once were alienated and enemies in your mind by wicked works, yet now He has reconciled in the body of His flesh through death, to present you holy, and blameless, and above reproach in His sight" (Col. 1:21–22). Hallelujah!

OFFER YOURSELF

The offerings, or at least portions of them, were burned on the brazen altar. When the very first offering was placed on the altar, the Lord Himself sent the fire that consumed it:

> Then Aaron lifted his hand toward the people, blessed them, and came down from offering the sin offering, the burnt offering, and peace offerings. And Moses and Aaron went into the tabernacle of meeting, and came out and blessed the people. Then the glory of the LORD appeared to all the people, and fire came out from before the LORD and consumed the burnt offering and the fat on the altar. When all the people saw it, they shouted and fell on their faces.
>
> —LEVITICUS 9:22–24

The glory of the Lord descended to the mercy seat, and the fire went out underneath the veil in front of the holy of holies and out into the outer court, all the way to the altar. Fire fell on the blood-soaked altar. Do you know what that tells me? If it's covered with the blood, the fire will fall on it. When it's covered with the blood, something is going to happen in the realm of no explanation and spread out beyond it. And do you know what the fire is? The fire is God's power and God's presence.

If you don't believe me, think back to what happened two thousand years ago on the day of Pentecost. The disciples were in the Upper Room in one accord. They had been freshly washed in the blood of Jesus Christ, and the Bible says,

> And suddenly there came a sound from heaven, as of a rushing mighty wind, and it filled the whole house where they were sitting. Then there appeared to them divided tongues, as of fire, and one sat upon each of them. And they were all filled with the Holy Spirit and began to speak with other tongues, as the Spirit gave them utterance.
>
> —ACTS 2:2–4

The disciples were washed in the blood, fire fell, and they were empowered by the Holy Spirit.

You don't have to be the right this or the right that, or have this title or that title, or do this thing or that thing to be empowered by the fire of God. If you're covered with the blood, the fire of the Holy Ghost will fall upon you and you will be empowered. Are you hungry for a fresh empowerment of the Holy Ghost? Are you ready for fresh fire? Let your proclamation of praise be a sign of your hunger. Tell the Lord, "God, I'm a candidate! I'm desperate for You! Let Your fire fall on me. I'm covered with the blood."

We talked about the sacrifices made on the altar in the Old Testament, under the Old Covenant. But we are under the New Covenant, and that brings us to a place where some people get uncomfortable. The altar had four horns, one on each corner. The horns of the altar were used to tie the sacrifice to the altar. The priests would take the sacrifice, come up the ramp, splatter the blood on the altar, and then tie the sacrifice to the altar. Psalm 118:27 says, "Bind the sacrifice with cords to the horns of the altar." I've often wondered why they needed to do that since the animals were killed before they were placed on the altar.

You don't have to be the right this or the right that to be empowered by the fire of God. If you're covered with the blood, the fire of the Holy Ghost will fall upon you and you will be empowered.

I think tying the sacrifices to the altar was foreshadowing a time when the sacrifices would be different. There is no need to sacrifice animals as burnt offerings, peace offerings, sin offerings, or trespass offerings anymore. Jesus took care of all that when He died on the cross. But the New Testament calls for a different kind of offering, a different kind of sacrifice: "I beseech you therefore, brethren, by the mercies of God, that you present your bodies a living sacrifice, holy, acceptable to God, which is your reasonable service" (Rom. 12:1).

We are called to be living sacrifices. The problem with living sacrifices is that they can crawl off the altar. A living sacrifice will say, "It's too hot; it's too hard," and try to get off the altar. But the sacrifice has to stay on the altar because it needs to be consumed. Understand what I'm trying to tell you: If you're not careful, the cares of life—the struggles, the issues, the trouble that you're going through—will cause you to want to crawl off the altar and say, "I just can't do this. I quit. It's too hard."

I'm going to be honest with you. There were times during the pandemic that I asked the Lord, "Can I do something else? This is hard. Trying to bring Your people together is hard." But I had to remind myself that I am a living sacrifice. So instead of saying, "Let me out of here," I need to say, "God, I will do whatever You ask of me. Tie me to Your altar. Tie me to Your will. Tie me to Your plan. Even if it gets hot, let me stay there. Even if it gets hard, let me stay there. I can't afford to get off Your altar."

This is what makes some people really uncomfortable or even scared. The thought of being wholly surrendered—a living sacrifice—day in and day out makes them really nervous. They think if they surrender completely to the will of God, they will end up somewhere in Outer Mongolia as a missionary.

But understand this, precious: Surrendering to the will of God for your life and offering yourself as a living sacrifice is the best thing you could ever do! And the truth is that God most likely will not send you to Outer Mongolia but instead will use you right where you are—with your family, your children, your neighbors, your coworkers, the girl in line behind you at the coffee shop, the guy at the next gas pump, and the cashier at the grocery store. You just need to be willing.

When you offer yourself as a living sacrifice, God does amazing things in you and through you. There is nothing like it. Is it hard? Absolutely! Is it worth it? Absolutely! So tie yourself to the altar. Some people are in trouble because they mess around and untie themselves from the altar. The devil can't untie you, but you can surely untie yourself. So if you've climbed off the altar, climb back up again and tie yourself to it. Allow yourself to be consumed by the power of God.

When you tie yourself to the altar, you're saying, "Lord, consume me. Consume my agenda, consume my attitudes, consume my compromise, consume my mind, consume my motivation, consume my life, consume my fears, consume my feelings of self-doubt, consume my past, consume my desires, consume my future, consume my pride, and consume anything in me that itches for glory. Don't let me get off Your altar. Let me stay on Your altar until I become what You intend for me to become." (And don't go getting mad at me if God sends you to Outer Mongolia. People there need to hear about Jesus too, and if God calls you to go there, He will equip you for the task.)

The sacrifice was consumed at the altar. That means agendas die at the altar. Compromises die at the altar. Sin, our own desires that separate us from God and cost us everything, lies on the altar and dies. Remember, the altar represents the cross. Jesus said to His disciples in Matthew 16:24, "If anyone desires to come after Me, let him deny himself, and take up his cross, and follow Me." Jesus was saying in essence, "As you go, take your altar with you." Your altar is not confined to a church, so take it with you. When you have your altar with you, everything changes. When you have your altar with you, it's hard to stay mad or offended. When you have your altar with you, it's hard to compromise, to sin, to lust.

The altar is a place where we bring an offering to God. And the offering God wants is you. Remember, He wants to connect with you. He wants to be in relationship with you so you can come boldly before His presence. Come to the altar when all you can offer is you. God isn't impressed by money or jewels or any other thing that you and I can bring Him. Yes, God is moved by your giving and your faithfulness, but in the end what He wants more than anything else is you.

So bring everything to the altar. Bring the good. Bring the bad. Bring the ugly. Bring your struggle. Bring your past. Bring your compromise. Bring that failure. Bring it all to the altar. But above all, bring you. Present yourself as a living sacrifice, holy and acceptable to God.

PRAYER

Lord, the altar is a place of repentance. It's where I confess my shortcomings. Lord, I present myself to You as a living sacrifice, holy and acceptable to You. I repent. Forgive me for anything in my life that grieves You. O God, see if there's any wicked way in me. Search my heart today, Lord. I present myself to You. I repent for division. I repent for compromise, attitudes, anger, and unforgiveness. I am sorry, God.

Lord, I thank You that Your sacrifice on the cross covered all my sin, all my trespasses, all my transgressions, and all my iniquities. Lord, I come to You just as I am, and I pray that You will consume anything in me that is not of You. I want Your will to be done in my life. I want to be wholly surrendered to You. I am a living sacrifice. Let me never crawl off the altar, in Jesus' name.

Chapter 4

THE LAVER

Christ also loved the church and gave Himself for her, that
He might sanctify and cleanse her with the washing of
water by the word, that He might present her to Himself
a glorious church, not having spot or wrinkle or any such
thing, but that she should be holy and without blemish.
—EPHESIANS 5:25–27

THE BRAZEN LAVER was the next piece of furniture in the wilderness tabernacle. It was placed between the brazen altar and the holy place. It was the place where the priest would wash himself and make himself clean before going into the holy place.

> Then the LORD spoke to Moses, saying: "You shall also make a laver of bronze, with its base also of bronze, for washing. You shall put it between the tabernacle

of meeting and the altar. And you shall put water in it, for Aaron and his sons shall wash their hands and their feet in water from it. When they go into the tabernacle of meeting, or when they come near the altar to min- ister, to burn an offering made by fire to the LORD, they shall wash with water, lest they die. So they shall wash their hands and their feet, lest they die. And it shall be a statute forever to them—to him and his descendants throughout their generations."

—EXODUS 30:17–21

The brazen laver is a place of sanctification. It's a place of cleansing. The journey to this point caused the priest to be in a position where he now needed to be cleansed. There are times when life puts us in situations where we need a fresh cleansing. Sometimes we need a fresh cleansing because of our own choices in life. Whatever the circumstances are that put you in need of cleansing, the brazen laver is the place to go for that cleansing.

The brazen laver was the place the priest would go because he was preparing to go to another dimension. He was pre- paring to go to another level. The priest was going to tran- scend the outer court and go into the inner court. And just as the priest was going to another level, you are too. God is getting ready to take you to another level. He's getting ready to take you to another dimension.

Let me ask you: Are you ready to go to another level, what- ever that looks like? Are you ready to go to a new dimension? You will need to leave some things behind to go to the next level. Are you ready to say, "I want to leave my past behind; I want to leave my frustrations behind; I want to leave my unforgiveness behind; I want to leave my compromise behind, and I want to go to a new dimension"? There are things that can exist at one level but can't make it to the next level. There are things that you have to leave at the altar, and there are things you need to be cleansed of at the laver. We all want to get to the realm of no explanation, to the miracles at the mercy seat, but we can't get to the miracles until we first go by the altar and then get cleansed at the laver.

You learned earlier that the brazen altar represents justification. The altar is where the blood flowed, meaning your sin is underneath the blood. While the altar represents justification, the brazen laver represents sanctification. *Sanctification* means to be set apart. When something is sanctified, it means it is set apart for the Master's use.

When the Lord washes you in the blood, when He justifies your life and then sets you apart, it means that He has a plan for you. It means that He wants to use you. It doesn't matter what people say about you. It doesn't matter what you have even said to yourself. Jesus still wants to use you.

We all want to get to the realm of no explanation, but we can't get to the miracles until we first go by the altar and then get cleansed at the laver.

He justified you so He can sanctify you and set you apart. This washing represents salvation. When Jesus washed you, He washed you clean.

THE MIRROR

The artisan in charge of building everything for inside the tabernacle was named Bezalel. The Lord "filled him with the Spirit of God, in wisdom, in understanding, in knowledge, and in all manner of workmanship, to design artistic works, to work in gold, in silver, in bronze, in cutting jewels for set-ting, in carving wood, and to work in all manner of work-manship" (Exod. 31:3–5). Since the laver was made of bronze, Bezalel was in charge of making it. The Bible says that "he made the laver of bronze and its base of bronze, from the bronze mirrors of the serving women who assembled at the door of the tabernacle of meeting" (Exod. 38:8).

Because the laver was made from the mirrors of the women who served at the door of the tabernacle, when the priest looked into the laver, he could see himself. He could see the reflection of himself in the bronze of the laver. He could see the dirt. He could see the mud. He could see the blood. And he would wash off all the dirt and blood because he was going to the next level, and he couldn't take all the dirt and blood with him. He was going into the holy place, and God's holiness is a big deal. God clearly warned, "They shall wash with water, lest they die" (Exod. 30:20). The priest knew the grime couldn't go with him, so he washed himself with the water in the laver.

The water in the laver represents the Word of God. Now, because Jesus has already died for our sins, anyone who has accepted Him as their Lord and Savior already has access straight into the presence of the Lord. The Bible says, "If we confess our sins, He is faithful and just to forgive us our sins and to cleanse us from all unrighteousness" (1 John 1:9). We can go "boldly to the throne of grace, that we may obtain mercy and find grace to help in time of need" (Heb. 4:16). But we still get dirty. We still get covered in grime. We still need to get cleaned up, especially when God is about to bring us to another level. And that is where the Word of God comes into play.

Ephesians 5:25–26 says, "Christ also loved the church and

gave Himself for her, that He might sanctify and cleanse her with the washing of water by the word." We looked at the meaning of that word *sanctify* earlier. It means to set apart. Jesus sets us apart, and He cleanses us with "the washing of water by the word."

The Greek word for washing used in the New Testament has the same root as the Greek word used for *laver*. The laver represents the Word of God. We look into the laver, the Bible, and it shows what we need to cleanse and why. It tells us how to live.

I know we're living in a day now when people don't want to live according to the Word of God. They think it's not good enough anymore. They think it is old-fashioned, out of date, and out of touch. Our generation thinks they know a better way. They think they have been enlightened and so know better than the God who created them. But if you want to be clean before God, you have to get out His Word and look in the mirror. You have to be cleansed by the washing of the water of the Word.

When you hold up the mirror of the Word to your life, don't just say, "Ooh, that part looks a little dirty," and walk away without doing anything about it. You need to do what the Word says, not just read it or hear it. The Bible says:

> But be doers of the word, and not hearers only, deceiving yourselves. For if anyone is a hearer of the word and not a doer, he is like a man observing his natural face in a mirror; for he observes himself, goes away, and immediately forgets what kind of man he was. But he who looks into the perfect law of liberty and continues in it, and is not a forgetful hearer but a doer of the work, this one will be blessed in what he does.
>
> —JAMES 1:22–25

If you looked in the mirror and saw a big blob of mud on your face, you wouldn't just walk away without cleaning it. So when you look into the mirror of the Word, clean off whatever you see. Don't go walking around with mud on your face. Be washed by the water of the Word of God. Get that Bible out and wash your life with it.

How Big?

Let's look again at the instructions about the laver the Lord gave to Moses:

> Then the LORD spoke to Moses, saying: "You shall also make a laver of bronze, with its base also of bronze, for washing. You shall put it between the tabernacle of meeting and the altar. And you shall put water in it, for Aaron and his sons shall wash their hands and their feet in water from it."
>
> —Exodus 30:17–19

God was very intentional and detailed in His instructions to Moses about the tabernacle. The Lord gave Moses specific dimensions for the tabernacle and its furniture—the coverings, the altar for burnt offerings, the altar of incense, the ark and the mercy seat, the table for the showbread, etc. But no measurements were given for the bronze laver. God allowed the people of Israel to make the laver as big or as small as they saw fit.

Since the laver represents the Word of God, that means we get to determine how big the Word is in our lives. So the question is, How big do you want the Word to be in your life?

God's Word is powerful. The Bible says, "For the word of God is living and powerful, and sharper than any two-edged sword, piercing even to the division of soul and spirit, and of joints and marrow, and is a discerner of the thoughts and intents of the heart" (Heb. 4:12). The Lord also said, "For as the rain comes down, and the snow from heaven, and do not return there, but water the earth, and make it bring forth and bud, that it may give seed to the sower and bread to the eater, so shall My word be that goes forth from My mouth; it shall not return to Me void, but it shall accomplish what I please, and it shall prosper in the thing for which I sent it" (Isa. 55:10–11). That means that God's Word is not only powerful, but it also will accomplish what God intended for it to accomplish.

You get to determine whether you believe the Word of God or you don't. Many saved folks are only surviving in the natural realm and have not tapped into the unlimited power of God's Word! But when you tap into God's Word, things change. There may not be a natural explanation for it, but something happens when you declare the Word of the Lord. When you start speaking the Word of the Lord, you're not saying what you said; you're saying what God said. When you speak His Word, you are declaring what the Lord said.

If I could tell you to do one thing in the season you are facing, it would be to start speaking the Word of God. The Word says, "Death and life are in the power of the tongue" (Prov. 18:21). You need to be speaking words of life, and there are no words of life more powerful than the living words from the Word of God.

Declare what God said about every situation. If you have lost children, say what God said about them. Don't say they'll never amount to anything. Don't declare that they're going to hell. Don't declare that they're losers. Those are words of death. Instead, begin to declare words of life over them. Declare that they are the head and not the tail and they are above and not beneath (Deut. 28:13). Say what God says about your family.

> But as for me and my house, we will serve the LORD.
> —JOSHUA 24:15

> But the mercy of the LORD is from everlasting to everlasting on those who fear Him, and His righteousness to children's children.
> —PSALM 103:17

> Behold, children are a heritage from the LORD, the fruit of the womb is a reward.
> —PSALM 127:3

Don't say what you see. Say what the Word of God says. And if you'll say what God said, you'll see what God said.

Say what God said about your health: "By His stripes I am healed. You are the Lord who heals me. Send out Your Word to heal me. Heal me, Lord, and I will be healed." (See Isaiah 53:5; Exodus 15:26; Psalm 107:20; Jeremiah 17:14.)

Say what God said about your money: "You are the Lord who provides. My God shall supply all my need according to His riches in glory by Christ Jesus. Because I seek the Lord, I shall not lack any good thing." (See Genesis 22:14; Philippians 4:19; Psalm 34:10.) You're not going to be broke, you're not going to be poor, because the name of the Lord gives you power to speak the Word of the Lord, and He will supply all of your needs.

Say what God said about your future. Don't say you're not going to amount to anything. Don't say you don't have a plan or a purpose or that you are lost. No, say: "God, You have a plan for me, to give me a future and a hope. All my days were written in Your book when as yet there were none of them. All things are working together for my good because I am called according to Your purpose. I have been called with a holy calling according to Your purpose and grace, which was given to me before time began." (See Jeremiah 29:11; Psalm 139:16; Romans 8:28; 2 Timothy 1:9.)

The key is to conform your life to what the Bible says. You are changed at the brazen laver. The living Word of God changes you from the inside out. That means, for example, you forgive even when you don't want to forgive because you know if you don't forgive your brothers and your sisters and your neighbors, then you can't claim the forgiving power of Jesus Christ in your life (Matt. 6:12).

The reality is that we have to live our lives at this laver. Remember, through justification at the altar and sanctification at the laver we are changed; we are set apart. We take a look in the mirror of the Word, and we do what that Bible says. And here's a truth you need to know: God will not judge us by what people think of us. He will not judge us by the opinions of others. He won't even judge us by what we think of ourselves. Instead, He will judge us by His Word. That is why it is so important that preachers continue to preach the Word.

We're living in a day when many preachers won't really preach the Word because they are afraid of people. They are afraid of what people will think or say if they teach the truth. They're afraid to stand up and really say what the Bible says. But I'll tell

> **At the brazen laver, the living Word of God changes you from the inside out.**

you the truth: I've been preaching the Word a long time, and I'm not afraid of what people will think or what people will do. I have the fear of the Lord, not fear of man. Proverbs 29:25 says, "The fear of man brings a snare." Fear of man is a trap. But "the fear of the LORD is the beginning of wisdom" (Prov. 9:10).

When you have the fear of the Lord, you want to preach His Word. You talk about the blood, you talk about redemption, you talk about sin, and you talk about salvation. You talk about the baptism and the gifts of the Holy Spirit. You don't run from issues; you stand up and talk about them.

So again, the question is, How big do you want the Word to be in your life?

WATER, BLOOD, AND OIL

When I was studying about the laver, I found out that the priest would splatter the blood, the anointing oil, and the water on the laver. Remember, the laver represents the Bible, the Word of God. So when the priest brought some of the blood from the brazen altar to the brazen laver, the laver was washed in the blood. You see, the Bible is a book of blood. Hallelujah! It's all about the blood. It is the blood that holds the Word together.

The priest would splatter the blood of a lamb on the laver. That is very powerful. It means when we read the Word, we read it washed in the blood of the Lamb—the precious blood of the Lamb of God who takes away the sins of the world. When you read the Bible, you don't have to read it in condemnation because there is no condemnation in Christ Jesus (Rom. 8:1). When you read the Word of the Lord, you don't have to read it in fear because God has given you free access to boldly approach Him (Heb. 4:16). You don't have to be afraid of the rapture or be afraid of hell because you are washed in the blood of the Lamb. Don't fear judgment, don't fear demons, and don't fear the devil—you are washed in the blood of the Lamb, and no weapon formed against you shall be able to prosper (Isa. 54:17).

So I read the Word of the Lord, and I draw close to God because I know I'm washed in the blood. I read about His return. I read about healing. I read about victory. I read about breakthrough. I read about mercy. I read about grace. I read about the power of God. Even when I read about judgment in the Bible, it doesn't pull me into condemnation because I've already been justified and sanctified.

In addition to the blood, the priest splattered the brazen laver with anointing oil. The anointing oil represents the Holy Spirit. So when you read your Bible, you don't read it in the flesh. You read it anointed in the Holy Ghost. Every time you read the Bible, read it with the knowledge that you are not only washed in the blood of the Lamb but also anointed by the Holy Ghost and can manifest the power of the Word of God in your life. Hallelujah!

That means in the mighty name of Jesus the anointing will break every yoke off your life and lift every burden. Even if something looks impossible, even if it looks like you cannot do it, you've been empowered by the Holy Spirit, so you can read that Bible and claim what it says as your own.

You are washed in the blood. You are anointed by the Holy Spirit. You are not anointed because you deserve it; you are anointed because you are washed in the blood. You are anointed because of who Jesus is and what Jesus has done. But we can't bypass the water. The water represents sanctification. It represents being set apart. It represents that part of you that is being transformed into His image.

Second Corinthians 3:18 says, "But we all, with unveiled face, beholding as in a mirror the glory of the Lord, are being transformed into the same image from glory to glory, just as by the Spirit of the Lord." You cannot ignore the Word of God and be changed into the image of God. His Word is key. It is a mirror. The brazen laver actually identified what needed to be cleansed. So when we look into the mirror and are washed by the water of the Word, it deals with the compromise. It deals with the anger. It deals with the unforgiveness. It deals with the sin.

Here is what I have found out after serving God all these years: We don't just read the Bible; the Bible reads us. The Bible shows us to ourselves. It's our mirror. Some of you have been looking in somebody else's mirror and trying to pattern your life after that person. Some of you have been using a code of ethics or a way of behavior, but in the end a worldly or politically correct code of ethics cannot justify you. It cannot sanctify you. You have to look to God's Word. It's His mirror. We get there, and we wash off our compromise. We wash off our sin. We wash off our past.

We don't just read the Bible; the Bible reads us.

I'll say it again: We don't just read the Bible; the Bible reads us. The Bible is absolute truth. That means it's always truth. The Bible is not relative truth. Relative truth says the truth changes relative to the situation that I'm in or how someone views it. Some might refer to it as situational ethics. But I'm telling you that the Bible is absolutely true. It is absolute truth. If the Bible says something is sin, then it is sin.

If something was sin in 1970, it's still sin today. It doesn't matter if it is now politically incorrect to call something—or anything—sin. Sin is sin.

That truth does not change, but neither does the truth that Jesus paid the price for sin, and He offers redemption, forgiveness, mercy, grace, and freedom—everything you need to live an abundant life in freedom and victory—to all who will repent and call upon the name of the Lord. This is absolute truth: "Whoever calls on the name of the LORD shall be saved" (Rom. 10:13).

The Bible is absolute, not obsolete. I know we have a lot of great communicators nowadays who stand on platforms and stages and communicate on TV. But we need more than good communicators. We need more than watered-down versions of the Word that won't offend anyone. We need preachers who will do more than just tell a nice story that makes you feel all warm and fuzzy but doesn't cause you to change, doesn't set you free, doesn't produce fruit in your life. We need preachers who will preach the Word until people get delivered, until the sick get healed, until marriages get restored, until lives are changed!

If we want to live in the realm of no explanation, we have to be rooted and grounded in the Word. The Bible is 100 percent true. "*All* Scripture is given by inspiration of God, and is profitable for doctrine, for reproof, for correction, for instruction in righteousness, that the man of God may be complete, thoroughly equipped for every good work" (2 Tim. 3:16–17, emphasis added). We don't get to cherry-pick the pieces and the parts we like and leave out the rest. We come to the laver and say, "Lord, sanctify me. Set me apart. Wash me, and I shall be clean."

The priest in the wilderness tabernacle was cleansed by

the word of the Lord. You might be thinking, "What does that have to do with me? I'm not a priest." But you are a priest. The Bible says, "But you are a chosen generation, *a royal priesthood*, a holy nation, His own special people, that you may proclaim the praises of Him who called you out of darkness into His marvelous light; who once were not a people but are now the people of God, who had not obtained mercy but now have obtained mercy" (1 Pet. 2:9–10, emphasis added).

You are part of the priesthood of the King of kings. That means you don't have to depend on a priest to intercede for you before the throne of God. You don't have to confess your sins to a man—although there are benefits to confessing your sin to another person, especially if you are stuck in habitual sin. "Confess your trespasses to one another, and pray for one another, that you may be healed" (Jas. 5:16). But as part of the royal priesthood of the Lord, you are now a priest, and when you come in the name of Jesus, you are ushered into the very presence of the Lord. You have been chosen as part of the royal priesthood.

In the tabernacle, the priest would cleanse himself to prepare to go to the next level. If he did not cleanse himself there, he would die. The priest was required to have a straight walk before the Lord. We are living in a day when the royal priesthood of God—that means everyone who is part of the body of Christ—needs to have a straight walk before the Lord. We especially need bishops, evangelists, pastors, teachers, and prophets who don't just preach the Word; they live it. I'm not saying they have to be perfect. But they need to be pursuing the Lord and to have a pure and straight walk before Him.

Come Clean

The priest washed his hands and his feet at the brazen laver. The feet represent every vile, illicit, immoral place that you have walked. Washing your feet represents being cleansed of the things you stepped in that you had no business stepping in. The feet represent the places you went that you had no business going. The feet represent where the priest had been polluted in the process, and he needed cleansing. Let me tell you something: Jesus' feet were nailed to the cross for every illicit place your feet have ever carried you.

The priest also washed his hands. Hands represent your actions, your deeds, the things you have done or haven't done. Psalm 24:3–5 says:

> Who may ascend into the hill of the LORD? Or who may stand in His holy place? He who has clean hands and a pure heart, who has not lifted up his soul to an idol, nor sworn deceitfully. He shall receive blessing from the LORD, and righteousness from the God of his salvation.

We need clean hands when we go before the Lord. We need to be cleansed of all our sinful actions. Washing your hands was a symbol of innocence in the Bible. Pilate, for example, when he tried to get the people to let him release Jesus but they called for His crucifixion instead, "took water and washed his hands before the multitude, saying, 'I am innocent of the blood of this just Person'" (Matt. 27:24). Washing his hands was a symbolic act declaring Pilate's innocence in the death of Jesus.

Just as Jesus' feet were nailed to the cross to atone for every vile place your feet have gone, His hands were nailed to the cross for every vile thing your hands have ever done. You can lift clean hands before the Lord in worship because the grace of God has wiped away every sin you have ever committed. His grace is sufficient for you (2 Cor. 12:9). "Though your sins are like scarlet, they shall be as white as snow; though they are red like crimson, they shall be as wool" (Isa. 1:18). Your clean hands are a symbol of your innocence in the sight of God, and that innocence was paid for in full by Jesus, who took all your guilt upon Himself.

The brazen laver is a reminder that it is time for you to come clean. Redeemed people must be clean people. You might be thinking, "I've already compromised. I've already gone too far. I'm so far gone into the ways of this world that there is no way back." Don't believe the lies of the enemy! There is no sin too big that God's grace isn't bigger still.

First John 1:9 says, "If we confess our sins, He is faithful and just to forgive us our sins and to cleanse us from all unrighteousness." God promises to forgive your sins when you confess them to Him. But He also promises to cleanse you from *all* unrighteousness. God doesn't want you walking around carrying your sin like an enormous burden that weighs you down and keeps you from walking in freedom. God wants you walking in freedom and victory, so come clean!

PRAYER

Lord, I come to Your laver, I come to Your Word, and I'm asking for You to sanctify me. I'm asking You to set me apart. I'm asking You to cover me by Your blood. I'm asking You to anoint me with the oil of Your Holy Spirit. I'm asking You to wash me with the water of Your Word. I am confessing my sins to you. Cleanse me from all unrighteousness.

God, let me get in Your Word, and let Your Word get in me. Renew my mind; renew my thinking. Drive out things that I've seen and heard that I shouldn't have. Change me by Your Word. Lord, wash me with Your Word. Whatever Your Word tells me to do, that's what I want to do. I want Your Word to be big in my life. I thank You for Your Word.

Lord, I declare that I have everything Your Word says I have. I declare that I am everything Your Word says I am. I declare that I can do anything Your Word says I can do. So I pray today, Lord, that Your Word would come alive in me. Order my steps in Your Word. I want to walk holy. I want to be holy. I want to be set apart. I want to be more like You. Conform me to Your image. Sanctify me through Your Word, Lord Jesus. Amen.

JimRaleyBooks.com/chp4

Chapter 5

THE FIVE PILLARS

And His name will be called Wonderful, Counselor,
Mighty God, Everlasting Father, Prince of Peace.
—Isaiah 9:6

AFTER THE PRIEST finished washing himself at the brazen laver, he was ready to go to the next level. He was ready to enter the holy place. Between the outer courtyard of the tabernacle and the holy place there was a door, a screen on five pillars. The Lord told Moses:

> You shall make a screen for the door of the tabernacle, woven of blue, purple, and scarlet thread, and fine woven linen, made by a weaver. And you shall make for the screen five pillars of acacia wood, and overlay them with gold; their hooks shall be gold, and you shall cast five sockets of bronze for them.
>
> —Exodus 26:36–37

The screen was another doorway, another indicator that you were moving closer to the presence of the Lord in the holy of holies, closer to the realm of no explanation. Three sides of the holy place were made of boards of acacia wood connected by silver sockets. But the entrance was different. It was five pillars of acacia wood, overlaid with gold, with a woven screen of blue, purple, and scarlet hung across them. Just like the blue, purple, and scarlet gate of the tabernacle looked different from the plain white linen hangings surrounding the rest of the tabernacle, the blue, purple, and scarlet screen on gold pillars looked different. It was marked as an entrance, a place to enter in.

Moses was specifically instructed that there should be five pillars for the screen into the holy place. We know that God is very intentional, so the number is not a random one. Five represents a lot in the Bible. There are five books in the Torah, or the Law: Genesis, Exodus, Leviticus, Numbers, and Deuteronomy. The Book of Psalms is divided into five smaller books. The Ten Commandments are divided into two sets of five: five commandments about our relationship with God, and five commandments about our relationship with each other. When Jesus fed the five thousand, He used five loaves (and two fish) to do it.

There are five types of offerings the children of Israel were commanded to bring before God: the burnt offering, the grain offering, the peace offering, the sin offering, and the trespass offering. The anointing oil used in the tabernacle had five ingredients: myrrh, cinnamon, sweet-smelling cane, cassia, and olive oil. And as we looked at earlier, five is the number of grace.

God could have chosen five pillars for any number of reasons. But in my opinion, it is a reminder of who He is.

Remember, the tabernacle is all about connection. God wants to connect to you, and He wants to be known by you. I think the five pillars are a reminder of the five facets of God's character revealed in a prophecy about Jesus in the Book of Isaiah. It's a familiar passage, often read at Christmastime:

> For unto us a Child is born, unto us a Son is given; and the government will be upon His shoulder. And His name will be called Wonderful, Counselor, Mighty God, Everlasting Father, Prince of Peace.
>
> —ISAIAH 9:6

The five pillars remind us of the five names of God in the verse, one name per pillar.[1] They tell us about who He is and how He wants to connect with us. They remind us of all that is possible in the realm of no explanation.

WONDERFUL

The first name of God in Isaiah 9:6 is Wonderful. This isn't the only time God is named as wonderful. In the Book of Judges, the Angel of the Lord (the preincarnate Jesus) appeared to Manoah to announce the birth of Samson. When Manoah asked the Angel His name, He replied, "Why do you ask My name, seeing it is wonderful?" (Judg. 13:18).

God is wonderful. It is not just how He is; it is *who* He is. In Hebrew, the word *wonderful* is *pele'*. It means miracle. It means a marvelous thing, something full of wonder.[2] I don't know about you, but I need a God of miracles. I need a God who does marvelous things. I need a God who works wonders. The Word says, "You are the God who does wonders; You have declared Your strength among the peoples" (Ps. 77:14). It also says, "O LORD, You are my God. I will exalt

You, I will praise Your name, for You have done wonderful things" (Isa. 25:1). God is definitely worthy of our praise for all the wonderful things He has done, the miracles, signs, and wonders.

But God doesn't just *do* wonderful things. He *is* wonderful. He is our Savior, our Redeemer. He loves us and knows each of us by name and the number of hairs on our heads. He is "God, ready to pardon, gracious and merciful, slow to anger, abundant in kindness" (Neh. 9:17). He is "a God full of compassion, and gracious, longsuffering and abundant in mercy and truth" (Ps. 86:15). "The name of the LORD is a strong tower; the righteous run to it and are safe" (Prov. 18:10). Nothing is too hard for Him (Jer. 32:17). "He is God, the faithful God who keeps covenant and mercy for a thousand generations with those who love Him and keep His commandments" (Deut. 7:9). And He "is the same yesterday, today, and forever" (Heb. 13:8). That means you can always count on Him, for He will be as wonderful today as He was yesterday, and He will be just as wonderful every day for all eternity. Is it any wonder His name is Wonderful?

COUNSELOR

The second name of the Lord in Isaiah 9:6 is Counselor. It is a title specifically given to the Holy Spirit in the New Testament:

> But the Counselor, the Holy Spirit, whom the Father will send in My name, will teach you everything and remind you of all that I told you.
>
> —JOHN 14:26, MEV

A counselor is someone who helps you, guides you, comforts you, gives you wisdom, teaches you, strengthens you, and supports you. A different version of the Bible translates the same verse in the Gospel of John this way:

> But the Helper (Comforter, Advocate, Intercessor—Counselor, Strengthener, Standby), the Holy Spirit, whom the Father will send in My name [in My place, to represent Me and act on My behalf], He will teach you all things. And He will help you remember everything that I have told you.
>
> —JOHN 14:26, AMP

I don't know about you, but I need the Holy Spirit as my Counselor. I need His help. I need His comfort. I need His guidance, His strength. I need Him to be advocating for me and interceding for me before the throne of grace. And in this crazy world we are living in, I need the wisdom of the Holy Spirit.

The Bible talks over and over again about the importance of wisdom and warns about foolishness. If you want to see some great examples of foolishness, just look on social media—you won't have to look very long. But wisdom—real wisdom—comes from God. Proverbs 2:6 says, "For the LORD gives wisdom." There is worldly wisdom of all kinds out there, all the -isms and -ologies and theories and everything else. But that isn't the wisdom you need. You need the real deal, the real thing.

First Corinthians 1:20 says, "Has not God made foolish the wisdom of this world?" God's wisdom makes the wisdom of the world look like complete foolishness. It's like comparing a doctoral thesis to the drawing of a puppy dog your preschooler colored. The puppy-dog drawing may look cute, but it is not going to help you make good decisions and good choices. Worldly wisdom may look good, but if it goes against what the Word says, it will just lead you to destruction. That's why we need the Holy Spirit, the Counselor.

The Book of Proverbs says, "Happy is the man who finds wisdom," and "Wisdom is better than rubies" (3:13; 8:11). I like the sound of that. Proverbs also says, "He who gets wisdom loves his own soul" (19:8). Getting wisdom sounds like a good idea—make that a wise idea. And do you know what is so great about the wisdom of the Lord? When you need it, all you have to do is ask! The Word says, "If any of you lacks wisdom, let him ask of God, who gives to all liberally and without reproach, and it will be given to him" (Jas. 1:5).

You need wisdom. I need wisdom. We all do. That is why we need the Counselor. I need to hear the Holy Spirit's voice leading me, redirecting me whenever I get off track.

> Your ears shall hear a word behind you, saying, "This is the way, walk in it," whenever you turn to the right hand or whenever you turn to the left.
>
> —ISAIAH 30:21

Now, the Hebrew word translated "Counselor" in Isaiah 9:6 is *yā'as*, meaning to advise, to counsel, to determine, to guide, or purpose.[3] Don't miss that the Holy Spirit's role as Counselor is tied to purpose. You have a unique purpose, a unique calling that God designed specifically for you. The Word says that you are "called according to His purpose" (Rom. 8:28). And if you want to walk fully in that purpose, you need the Counselor; you need the wisdom, guidance, counsel, and comfort of the Holy Spirit.

MIGHTY GOD

The third name of the Lord in Isaiah 9:6 is Mighty God. I love this part of God's character. I don't serve some wimpy, do-nothing, scaredy-cat God. I serve the Lord God Almighty, Maker of heaven and earth. Great and marvelous are His works; just and true are His ways (Rev. 15:3). He is the Lord God Omnipotent, which means He is all-powerful. There is nothing too hard for Him (Gen. 18:14; Jer. 32:17). The Lord my God "is God of gods and Lord of lords, the great God, mighty and awesome" (Deut. 10:17). I have seen His greatness, His wonders. I have seen the power of His mighty hand and outstretched arm. He is Mighty God!

The Hebrew word for mighty in Isaiah 9:6 is *gibôr*. It means strong, powerful, warrior, champion, giant, powerful, and valiant.[4] It is actually an intensive form of the Hebrew word *geber*, which means strong man or warrior.[5] When a word is intensive, it means it is a stronger, more intense, more concentrated form of the word. That means that when the Word says God is mighty, it means He is intensely mighty, super mighty, 100 percent mighty.

I don't know about you, but I need our Mighty God. We are in a fierce battle, as I'm sure you've noticed. The enemy is waging war against us—against the church, against families, against marriages, against children, against the truth, against anything that will further the kingdom of God on the earth. And we need to do our part in the battle. We need to fight back against the enemy.

When the Word says God is mighty, it means He is intensely mighty, super mighty, 100 percent mighty.

We need to put on the whole armor

of God and stand fast against the schemes and tricks of the devil. We need to raise up our shields of faith and wield our swords of the Spirit—the Word of God—skillfully and strategically. We need to speak the truth in love and stand up for the truth. But ultimately the battle isn't ours. Yes, we need to fight, but we need to fight on our knees, going boldly before the throne of grace to find help in time of need. We need to fight by lifting up our voices in worship even in the midst of the fiercest battle. We need to fight by wiping out every lie the enemy fires at us with the truth of the Word of God. And we must never forget the battle belongs to the Lord.

You may feel like your situation is hopeless. You may feel messed up from the chest up, beat up from the feet up, and tore up from the floor up. What you are facing may seem like a giant. But never forget, precious, that we serve the Mighty God! When King David was facing battle with the giant Goliath, he wasn't trusting in a king's armor to save him. He wasn't trusting in a sword or a spear. He wasn't even trusting in his little slingshot and the five smooth stones he plucked out of the brook. He was trusting in the Lord, for He is Mighty God. David told Goliath:

> You come to me with a sword, with a spear, and with a javelin. But I come to you in the name of the LORD of hosts, the God of the armies of Israel, whom you have defied. This day the LORD will deliver you into my hand....Then all this assembly shall know that the LORD does not save with sword and spear; for the battle is the LORD's, and He will give you into our hands.
>
> —1 SAMUEL 17:45–47

And that is exactly what the Lord did. The giant who defied the Lord went tumbling to the ground, dead as a doornail, not because David was good with a slingshot but because David knew who was really fighting the battle. The battle is the Lord's. He is Mighty God, and there is no battle that He cannot win. He is the "King of glory...the LORD strong and mighty, the LORD mighty in battle" (Ps. 24:8).

So when the enemy comes against you, trying to make you think he has already won the battle and your children will always be lost, your marriage will always be a mess, your money will always be funny, or you will always be in bondage to your habits, your hiccups, and your hang-ups, you just shut him right up with the truth. Say, "I serve the Mighty God! The battle belongs to Him. Devil, you have already lost! I have been redeemed by the finished work of Jesus on the cross, and I am going to walk in the freedom Jesus died to give me! You may think you have won, but I know the truth. There may be giants in my life right now, but God is going to take them out. He is Mighty God, and there is nothing too hard for Him!"

EVERLASTING FATHER

The fourth name of the Lord in Isaiah 9:6 is Everlasting Father. This is an important one, precious. God is our Father.

Fathers are important. Good fathers provide security, a sense of well-being, protection, discipline, support, comfort, and countless other important things in our lives. Fatherlessness is epidemic in our society, and we are seeing the fallout. We all have heard the statistics. Children who grow up without fathers are more likely to drop out of school, live in poverty, be victims of abuse or neglect, go to prison, abuse drugs or alcohol, have behavior problems, etc.[6] And unfortunately it is not just the lack of fathers, but also fathers who neglect, abuse, mistreat, or ignore their children that are part of the problem.

Because of father-related problems, there are countless people walking around with father wounds. They feel rejected, afraid, insecure, uncertain, and unloved. And those father wounds often make it difficult for people to relate to God as their Father because their experiences with their earthly fathers were not good ones. If someone was mistreated or ridiculed for asking for help from their father, they might be afraid to boldly approach the throne of grace to find help because they fear God will do the same. People may struggle to believe they are accepted by the Lord because they were rejected by their fathers. They may be scared to trust God because their fathers were untrustworthy. They may wonder if it is safe to love the Lord because they loved their fathers but were abused by them. The wounds can run so deep.

Precious, if you are one of those people with father wounds, I need you to hear me: God is not like your father. He is a good Father, a perfect Father. Isaiah 9:6 describes Him as the Everlasting Father. *Everlasting* means forever. God is not going to leave you. He is not going to abandon you. Deuteronomy 31:6 says, "Be strong and of good courage, do not fear nor be afraid of them; for the LORD your God, He is the One who goes with you. He will not leave you nor forsake you." Hebrews 13:5 says, "For He Himself has said, 'I will never leave you nor forsake you.'"

When Jesus gave the Great Commission to the disciples, He said, "I am with you always, even to the end of the age" (Matt. 28:20). Those are just some of the promises of God that let you know that Father God, the Everlasting Father, will not ever leave you. And we know that "all the promises of God in Him are Yes, and in Him Amen, to the glory of God through us" (2 Cor. 1:20).

The Hebrew word translated "Father" in Isaiah 9:6 is *'āḇ*. It is the first word alphabetically in the Hebrew language, and while its most basic meaning is father, it means so much more. It is a term of protection, of benevolence. It can mean author, maker, or creator. It can refer to someone who nourishes or brings up a child. It can mean master or teacher. It is used "to express intimate connection and relationship."[7] Precious, that is the kind of Father the Lord is.

He is your protector, your shield, your place of refuge.

> Do not be terrified, or afraid of them. The LORD your God, who goes before you, He will fight for you, according to all He did for you in Egypt before your eyes, and in the wilderness where you saw how the LORD your God carried you, as a man carries his son, in all the way that you went until you came to this place.
> —DEUTERONOMY 1:29–31

> My sheep hear My voice, and I know them, and they follow Me. And I give them eternal life, and they shall never perish; neither shall anyone snatch them out of My hand. My Father, who has given them to Me, is greater than all; and no one is able to snatch them out of My Father's hand.
> —JOHN 10:27–29

He is a kind, gracious, benevolent Father.

> If you then, being evil, know how to give good gifts to your children, how much more will your Father who is in heaven give good things to those who ask Him!
> —MATTHEW 7:11

Look at the birds of the air, for they neither sow nor reap nor gather into barns; yet your heavenly Father feeds them. Are you not of more value than they?

—MATTHEW 6:26

Every good gift and every perfect gift is from above, and comes down from the Father of lights, with whom there is no variation or shadow of turning.

—JAMES 1:17

He is the Father who created you, who designed you, who made you on purpose and with purpose.

But now, O LORD, You are our Father; we are the clay, and You our potter; and all we are the work of Your hand.

—ISAIAH 64:8

For You formed my inward parts; You covered me in my mother's womb. I will praise You, for I am fearfully and wonderfully made; marvelous are Your works, and that my soul knows very well. My frame was not hidden from You, when I was made in secret, and skillfully wrought in the lowest parts of the earth. Your eyes saw my substance, being yet unformed. And in Your book they all were written, the days fashioned for me, when as yet there were none of them.

—PSALM 139:13–16

He is the Father who wants to bless you, help you grow, heal your wounds, and be the Father you never had.

A father of the fatherless...is God in His holy habitation.

—PSALM 68:5

As a father shows compassion to his children, so the
LORD shows compassion to those who fear him.
—PSALM 103:13, ESV

Blessed be the God and Father of our Lord Jesus Christ,
who has blessed us with every spiritual blessing in the
heavenly places in Christ, just as He chose us in Him
before the foundation of the world, that we should be
holy and without blame before Him in love, having
predestined us to adoption as sons by Jesus Christ to
Himself, according to the good pleasure of His will, to
the praise of the glory of His grace, by which He made
us accepted in the Beloved.
—EPHESIANS 1:3–6

He is the Father who will teach you the ways of wisdom,
discipline you with love (not abuse), and guide you on correct paths.

Do not despise the chastening of the LORD, nor detest
His correction; for whom the LORD loves He corrects,
just as a father the son in whom he delights.
—PROVERBS 3:11–12

And above all else, He is the Everlasting Father who longs
to have a close, intimate relationship with you, His precious
son or daughter.

For you did not receive the spirit of bondage again to
fear, but you received the Spirit of adoption by whom
we cry out, "Abba, Father." The Spirit Himself bears witness with our spirit that we are children of God.
—ROMANS 8:15–16

> Behold what manner of love the Father has bestowed on
> us, that we should be called children of God!
>
> —1 JOHN 3:1

The Everlasting Father, who is perfect in all His ways, wants connection with you. Let Him be the Father you need.

PRINCE OF PEACE

The last name of the Lord in Isaiah 9:6 is Prince of Peace. I am telling you that I need the Prince of Peace in this crazy world we are living in. I need the Prince of Peace because I need real peace. I don't need peace the world offers, when you pretend all your worries and cares and troubles aren't there, or when you drown your troubles with alcohol or get high to forget for a little while, or where you do anything and everything just to try not to feel anything. I need the real deal, the peace that comes from God alone.

The Hebrew word translated "Prince" in Isaiah 9:6 is *śar*. It means prince, captain, keeper, chief, or ruler.[8] This means God is the One who is in charge of real peace. He is its keeper, its captain, its chief.

The word translated "Peace" is *šālôm*, or *shalom*. Shalom is real peace. It means completeness, wholeness, welfare, safety, security, prosperity, health, happiness, tranquility, contentment, friendship, and peace.[9] This is true peace. This is real peace. It isn't shallow or temporary. It is the knowledge that you rest safely in the arms of a gracious Father who protects and provides, who battles for you and blesses you, who loves you and loves to be with you. This is the peace that passes all understanding.

Philippians 4:6–7 says, "Be anxious for nothing, but in

everything by prayer and supplication, with thanksgiving, let your requests be made known to God; and the peace of God, which surpasses all understanding, will guard your hearts and minds through Christ Jesus." Precious, the peace of God guards your heart and your mind. It helps protect your heart from those who would seek to wound it, and when you do get wounded, it helps your heart to heal.

The peace of God can protect your mind from all the lies the world tells you and the lies the enemy tries to get you to believe. The peace of God isn't dependent on your circumstances. When you are in a storm or a fire or a pandemic, or just the everyday troubles of life, turn to the Prince of Peace. Lay your cares and

God is the One who is in charge of real peace. He is its keeper, its captain, its chief.

your troubles and your worries at His feet. Know that He is Wonderful, Counselor, Mighty God, Everlasting Father, and Prince of Peace. Rest in Him.

The five pillars in the tabernacle were there to hold something up. It kept something from folding in, from collapsing, from ending up in a crumpled heap on the ground. And the One who is called Wonderful, Counselor, Mighty God, Everlasting Father, and Prince of Peace is holding you up. He is holding up your life, your world. He is holding it all together.

Isaiah 9:6 says that "the government will be upon His shoulder," but it doesn't stop there. Your family is on His shoulder. Your ministry is on His shoulder. Your future is on His shoulder. You are on His shoulder. The Lord, who is everything we talked about in this chapter and more, loves you beyond your wildest imagination, and He wants to be connected to you so you can enter the realm of no explanation.

PRAYER

Lord, You are wonderful. Jesus, don't let me ever lose sight of the wonder that You are. Don't let me ever lose sight of how wonderful and awesome and precious You are. Lord, You are the God who does wonders! There's nobody like You. I praise Your name, for You have done wonderful things.

I praise You, Lord, for sending the Holy Spirit as my Counselor. Thank You, Lord, for Your wisdom, Your guidance, and Your comfort. Fill me continually with Your wisdom, Lord, because I need it. I need to hear Your voice saying, "This is the way, walk in it." Thank You, Lord, for keeping me on the right path, for guiding me according to Your purpose for my life.

You are Mighty God. Be Mighty God in my life. Be Mighty God in my nation. O God, I thank You that You are the Mighty God. I thank You for showing Yourself strong on my behalf. You are my shield, my protector, my defender, and nothing is too hard for You. I thank You that You are mightier than the enemy. I thank You that You are mightier than sin. You are mightier than compromise. I give You praise that You are mightier than the agenda of hell.

You are the Everlasting Father. You are my Everlasting Father. Lord, You always have been and You always will be. I pray that I will see Your goodness as the Everlasting Father revealed. People may have abandoned me and forsaken me, but You have been constant. Heal my father wounds with Your love,

Your grace, and Your goodness. You are the Everlasting Father, and I give You praise for it.

Lord, You are the Prince of Peace, and I am praying for peace today. Lord, I need true peace. I need Your peace. I pray for peace for my family. I pray for peace for my church. I pray for peace for my nation. You're the Prince of Peace. I pray that Your peace would take hold of Your people. I give You praise for Your peace that passes all understanding. Lord, You are Wonderful, Counselor, Mighty God, Everlasting Father, Prince of Peace!

JimRaleyBooks.com/chp5

Chapter 6

THE GOLDEN LAMPSTAND

*Then Jesus spoke to them again, saying, "I am the
light of the world. He who follows Me shall not
walk in darkness, but have the light of life."*
—JOHN 8:12

THE PRIEST STARTED outside and entered the gates with
praise and thanksgiving. He went to the altar, representing justification, and the brazen laver, representing sanctification. He then passed through the five pillars: Wonderful,
Counselor, Mighty God, Everlasting Father, and Prince of
Peace. And when the priest passed through the blue, scarlet,
and purple screen on the five pillars, he went to another level.
He entered the holy place.

When the priest entered the holy place, he would see the
golden lampstand on his left, the table of showbread on the
right, and the altar of incense in front of him. As with all the

furniture in the tabernacle, God gave specific instructions to Moses about the lampstand:

> You shall also make a lampstand of pure gold; the lampstand shall be of hammered work. Its shaft, its branches, its bowls, its ornamental knobs, and flowers shall be of one piece. And six branches shall come out of its sides: three branches of the lampstand out of one side, and three branches of the lampstand out of the other side. Three bowls shall be made like almond blossoms on one branch, with an ornamental knob and a flower, and three bowls made like almond blossoms on the other branch, with an ornamental knob and a flower—and so for the six branches that come out of the lampstand. On the lampstand itself four bowls shall be made like almond blossoms, each with its ornamental knob and flower. And there shall be a knob under the first two branches of the same, a knob under the second two branches of the same, and a knob under the third two branches of the same, according to the six branches that extend from the lampstand. Their knobs and their branches shall be of one piece; all of it shall be one hammered piece of pure gold. You shall make seven lamps for it, and they shall arrange its lamps so that they give light in front of it. And its wick-trimmers and their trays shall be of pure gold. It shall be made of a talent of pure gold, with all these utensils. And see to it that you make them according to the pattern which was shown you on the mountain.
>
> —EXODUS 25:31–40

The golden lampstand is very powerful. The golden lampstand points us to the Lord. First John 1:5 says, "God is light and in Him is no darkness at all." The golden lampstand points us to Jesus because Jesus said in John 8:12, "I am the light of the world." Aren't you so thankful that you know the Light of the world? The Light of the world is not Independent, Democrat, or Republican. The Light of the world is not a governor or a president that is elected. The Light of the world is the King of kings and Lord of lords. He's unstoppable and unfathomable, and there's no light like Him. Everything else pales in comparison. The lampstand points us to Jesus.

SEVEN LAMPS

The lampstand had three branches coming off the center shaft of the lampstand on each side, so there were a total of seven lamps. On the top of each branch was a bowl shaped like an almond blossom, which held the lamp. The lamps and the lampstand were hollow, and the priest would take pure olive oil and pour it in. The priests were in charge of making sure the lamps stayed lit.

> And you shall command the children of Israel that they bring you pure oil of pressed olives for the light, to cause the lamp to burn continually. In the tabernacle of meeting, outside the veil which is before the Testimony, Aaron and his sons shall tend it from evening until morning before the LORD. It shall be a statute forever to their generations on behalf of the children of Israel.
> —EXODUS 27:20–21

The seven individual lamps represent the seven churches in the Book of Revelation. And so the lampstand points to the church. The lampstand was the only source of light in the holy place, and the oil is what made the lamp a source of light. The lamp was nothing without the oil. You couldn't see anything in the holy place without the oil. You would lose your way without the oil. You couldn't find what you needed without the oil.

In the Bible, the oil represents the Holy Spirit. It represents the anointing. And just as the olive oil was necessary for the lampstand, the oil of the Holy Spirit is necessary for the church. It doesn't matter how nice your church building is; it doesn't matter how good your music is; it doesn't matter how well-spoken your pastor is; it doesn't matter how many people go to your church—if you don't have the oil of the Holy Spirit in your church, you will lose your way. The church needs the oil because the oil produces the fire. The church has been trying to produce fire without oil, but it cannot be done.

The priest took his job seriously. He tended to the flame. He took responsibility for the flame. He trimmed the lamps morning and evening, trimming the wicks with the gold wick-trimmers Moses was instructed to make and replenishing the oil. It was important that the priest trim the wicks to keep soot from developing and causing the lamps to smoke. Why? Because there was no smoke allowed in the holy place. God said, "I don't want anything in the holy place that would stop you from seeing the bread. I don't want anything in the holy place that would hinder you from seeing what I have for you to see. So you have to see to it now. You have to be careful with it. You have to keep the lamps burning cleanly."

The church needs the oil because the oil produces the fire. The church has been trying to produce fire without oil, but it cannot be done.

I would tell preachers reading this, you'd better watch your life. You'd better watch how you live. You'd better watch what you let in your ministry. You'd better watch what you let in your church. You'd better watch what you allow to stand on that stage. We have to burn clean. If there are things smoking up your church, you need to start trimming. The church must have a pure flame and clean oil.

YOU NEED A SOURCE

Even though multiple translations of the Bible—the King James Version, for example—call the lampstand a candlestick, it did not use candles. When a candle burns, it consumes itself. A candle depends on itself for fuel, and once the candle melts, once all the wax melts, the candle goes out. A lamp is different, which is why the lampstand didn't have candles. The light in the holy place came from lamps filled with oil. The lamps needed an outside source to provide their oil.

The golden lampstand had oil and fire, representing anointing and empowerment for the believer—and we all need the anointing and empowerment of the Holy Spirit. I want God's power in my life. I would rather have God's power than your endorsement. I'd rather have God's power than man's applause. I'd rather have God's power than anything else because I know that when I'm empowered by the Holy Ghost, I have the power to burn demons and devils. I have the power to release healing, miracles, signs, and wonders. I don't just want to know the Word; I want to be empowered to fulfill the Word. I want to be able to see signs and wonders and miracles manifest in my life.

The lampstand points us to the power of God. But as a lamp burns, it consumes the oil it is using for fuel. That is why the lamps needed a continual replenishing of oil, morning and evening. They needed a source outside themselves in order to keep burning.

You need a source outside yourself to keep burning too. You are not your own source. You need a continual replenishing of the oil of the Holy Ghost. You need to be continually refilled by the Holy Ghost's power if you expect to continue burning. You need the oil.

If you don't have the oil in your life, you'll say yes to the wrong things. If you don't have the oil in your life, you'll marry the wrong man. If you don't have the oil in your life, you'll make wrong decisions. If you don't have the oil in your life, you will burn out.

I'll be honest with you. There have been many times I would have burned out if I had been trying to be my own source. There have been many times when I would have quit.

God has called you to be not a candle but a lamp. To keep burning, you are dependent on the oil of the Holy Spirit.
There have been many times I would have walked away and said, "I can't do this anymore." In 2020 it got particularly rough. But let me tell you something: I was not consuming myself. I was not my own source. There was an outside source. The oil of the Spirit gave me power. I know that if I continually refill my life with the power of the Holy Spirit in fresh oil, I will continue to burn.

While Jesus said, "I am the light of the world" (John 8:12), He also said, "You are the light of the world" (Matt. 5:14). He is the Light of the world, and when you spend time with Him, you are going to become the light of the world. When you hang out with Jesus, He is going to set you on fire. God has called you to be not a candle but a lamp. To keep burning, you are dependent on the oil of the Holy Spirit.

TRIAL BY FIRE

The lampstand was made of gold and weighed about seventy-five pounds. It was priceless because the gold had been refined by fire and hammered and molded into a beautiful lampstand. Gold ore isn't worth as much when it is first found. It is the process of being refined by fire and molded and hammered into shape that prepares it and adds value to it. The gold didn't become valuable until it went through the fire. The gold didn't become valuable until it got hammered. It didn't become valuable until it went through something. It was prepared, and what it went through did not diminish it; it added value to it.

Some of you have gone through some things. You've had long days and lonely nights. You wept and cried and prayed, and things didn't go the way you wanted them to go. You've been through trials. You've been hurt. You've been wounded. But here is what hell doesn't want you to know: The fire that you went through has only added value to you. Your struggle has only added value to you. It has made you even more precious than you already were. In 1 Peter 4:12 the Bible refers to trials as "fiery." Thank God that you went through the fire because you are coming out of it as pure gold.

Let me speak to you from my heart, precious. It was the fire that got the lampstand ready for the oil. We have all been through some trying seasons recently. It seems the enemy has been producing one fiery trial after another. Some of you have been through one thing and then another and then another. The problems and issues have seemed never-ending. But the trials have not been in vain. The devil is panicking right now because he knows your fire has prepared you to receive fresh oil. Hallelujah! I declare we are coming out of our trials with fresh oil, and we will be set on fire for the things of God!

BY THE NUMBERS

The center shaft of the golden lampstand had things called knobs that held everything together. There were three knobs, one under the first two branches, one under the second two branches, and one under the third two branches. The three knobs held together the seven branches. Three represents the Godhead, and the Godhead is the foundation of the church.

This is a key concept. The Godhead needs to be our foundation. We're not going to see revival in this next season if we are building on our personalities. We're not going to see revival if we are building on good music. We're not going to see revival because we have a nice building. We need a last-days revival that will rescue your children. I want you to understand that fire will fall and glory will come when we build on the presence of God the Father, God the Son, and God the Holy Ghost.

Each side branch of the lampstand had three ornaments made up of three parts: a bowl shaped like an almond blossom, an ornamental knob, and a flower. Almond trees are the first ones to blossom every spring in Israel, so the almond blossom is a symbol of new life, of resurrection, of renewal, of hope, and of a fresh start. I don't know about you, but there are times I need a reminder that in Jesus I have new life and hope and a chance to start again because of His glorious grace and forgiveness.

Notice that there were nine ornaments on each side of the lampstand. Nine ornaments on one side represent the fruit of the Spirit: "But the fruit of the Spirit is love, joy, peace, longsuffering, kindness, goodness, faithfulness, gentleness, self-control" (Gal. 5:22–23). Nine ornaments on the other side represent the gifts of the Spirit: "Now concerning spiritual gifts, brethren, I do not want you to be ignorant....for to one is given the word of wisdom through the Spirit, to another the word of knowledge through the same Spirit, to another faith by the same Spirit, to another gifts of healings by the same Spirit, to another the working of miracles, to another prophecy, to another discerning of spirits, to another different kinds of tongues, to another the interpretation of tongues" (1 Cor. 12:1, 8–10).

Remember that the branches represent the church. The church needs the fruit of the Spirit, and the church needs the gifts of the Spirit. If we are going to be the light of the world, we need love. We need joy. We need peace and all the other fruit that makes the world take notice and ask, "Why are you so loving when people are so mean? Why do you have joy when you are going through a trial? Why do you have peace when the world is going crazy?"

If the church is going to be the light of the world, we need people to be operating in their gifts of the Spirit. The Word says, "But the manifestation of the Spirit is given to each one for the profit of all" (1 Cor. 12:7). We need people gifted with the word of wisdom to be speaking wisdom. We need people with the gift of faith to be exercising it in mighty ways. We need people with the gifts of healings and miracles to be manifesting the supernatural in the church and in the world. Whatever gift or gifts you have, you need to be using them as the Spirit directs, for the benefit of everyone and for the glory of God.

If you add up the number of bowls, knobs, and flowers in the ornaments on the central shaft and the branches, the total is sixty-six. There are no accidents. It didn't just happen to be that way. Everything about the tabernacle tells us there's more to come. And the sixty-six bowls, knobs, and flowers point us straight to the Word of God, for there are sixty-six books in the Bible.

Don't miss this: The sixty-six ornaments are part of a lampstand that gives light so you can see the table of showbread. The Bible says, "Man shall not live by bread alone; but man lives by every word that proceeds from the mouth of the LORD" (Deut. 8:3). Jesus Himself quoted that verse when the devil was tempting Him. The Bible also says, "Your word is a lamp to my feet and a light to my path" (Ps. 119:105). The Word of God is itself a light, a lamp. And that light points you straight to the bread, which also represents the Word.

We need the light so we can see the bread. But here's the problem: Have you ever been to church before and the preacher is preaching and declaring and talking, but you don't know what he's saying? He stands up there and says, "You're suffering from a dramatic dislocation of your emotional processes. Your inability to cope with reality is due to a massive inferiority complex because your mother dropped you on your head when you were a small child, and it has transcended and now you are struggling with that issue even yet today." And you're sitting there scratching your head because you don't know what in the world the man just said. He didn't preach a message; he gave a little talk.

Well, I'm not that kind of preacher. Your mama may have dropped you on your head when you were a little boy, but I know a God that can heal your head. That God can save your mama, that God can take care of issues, and that God can turn your life around. The problem is that some preachers are preaching but there's no oil in the house, there's no light in the house, and nobody can see the bread. But let me tell you, when you get oil in the house and you get fire in the house, you can see the bread. And you know what? I want the bread. Show me the bread! Don't just preach me a good message. Don't just chill me and thrill me. Teach me a message covered in the oil burning with fire. Get me to the bread.

The lampstand had no measurements. That points to the unlimited impact of the light and its ability to overcome darkness. Speaking of Jesus the Bible says, "In the beginning was the Word, and the Word was with God, and the Word was God. He was in the beginning with God. All things were made through him, and without him was not any thing made that was made. In him was life, and the life was the light of men. The light shines in the darkness, and the darkness has not overcome it" (John 1:1–5, ESV).

Jesus is the living Word. He brings life, and that life brings light. He is the Light of the world. And because we have Jesus, we too are the light of the world. Our job as the church is to produce light in a dead world. Our job is to bring life to a dead world. Our job is to bring hope to the hopeless, joy to the despairing, peace to the tormented. But to do that, we need the oil. We need the fire. We need the Light.

Some of you have been so afraid. You say, "Oh, it's getting dark; it's getting darker and darker." Let me tell you something: The light shines the brightest in the darkness. You can be in the deepest, darkest cave, far underground, where there is absolutely no natural light, and one little match will light the place up. Light always shines in the darkness. Darkness cannot shut off a light or snuff a candle or put out a lamp.

I believe this is the church's finest hour. Our job is not to sit around and complain and act like we're full of fear. Our job is to produce light in a dark world. I wouldn't give you ten cents for a life that did not shine, and I'm telling you, we are going to shine in these days. We are going to be the light. The light shines in the darkness, and the darkness has not, cannot, and will not overcome it!

PRAYER

Lord, I raise up my hands to You today. Let me burn clean oil. Give me clean hands and a pure heart. Don't let my light produce smoke. Lord, have Your way in me. I'm asking for Your light to shine on me. I'm asking for Your Word to be a lamp to my feet and a light to my path. There is no darkness in You, and I don't want there to be any darkness in me. I need Your oil. Fill me with the Holy Spirit, Lord. Anoint me with Your Spirit. Lord, You are my source. I don't want or need another. I may be facing fiery trials, but I will come out with fresh oil and set on fire for You. Because You are the Light of the world, I will be the light of the world. And the darkness will never overcome the light! Thank You, Jesus!

JimRaleyBooks.com/chp6

Chapter 7

THE TABLE OF SHOWBREAD

And you shall set the showbread on
the table before Me always.
—Exodus 25:30

THE GOLDEN LAMPSTAND lit the way to the table of showbread. The bread represents both the Word of God and the presence of God. Moses's instructions for the table of showbread were as follows:

> You shall also make a table of acacia wood; two cubits shall be its length, a cubit its width, and a cubit and a half its height. And you shall overlay it with pure gold, and make a molding of gold all around. You shall make for it a frame of a handbreadth all around, and you shall make a gold molding for the frame all around. And you shall make for it four rings of gold, and put the rings on the four corners that are at its four legs. The rings shall

be close to the frame, as holders for the poles to bear the table. And you shall make the poles of acacia wood, and overlay them with gold, that the table may be carried with them. You shall make its dishes, its pans, its pitchers, and its bowls for pouring. You shall make them of pure gold. And you shall set the showbread on the table before Me always.

—Exodus 25:23–30

Notice the description of the table includes "a molding of gold all around" (v. 24). It's as if the table has a crown. The table of showbread is actually the first place that we see a crown in the tabernacle. To me, a crown speaks of importance, and I'm telling you that there is nothing more important in your life than the bread of God's presence and the bread of God's Word.

IN THE PRESENCE OF MY ENEMIES

The Bible talks a lot about tables. A table is a place to relax and enjoy a meal. It's a place to sit and talk to others face to face, forging connections and developing relationships. It's a place of nourishment—physically, emotionally, and spiritually. Remember, the Lord wants to connect with you. He wants you to spend time in His presence. So no matter the circumstances you are facing, He is inviting You to the table. He is inviting you to be refreshed by His presence and by feasting on His Word. He is inviting you to connect with Him.

Psalm 23:5 says, "You prepare a table before me in the presence of my enemies." That means even when enemies are surrounding you on every side, even when you are in the wilderness, even when you are in the midst of a fierce battle, God has a table prepared for you. He has prepared a place for you to rest in His presence and feast on His Word. Even when it's a struggle and people are starving to death all around you, the Lord said He will prepare a table for you.

God will prepare a table for you right in the presence of all those haters—and all those haters, those people who said you wouldn't make it, those people who said there was no hope for you, those people who tried to beat you up and beat you down, are going to have to watch you eat. They are going to have a front-row seat to your Savior and Redeemer blessing you with His presence and filling you with His Word. They said you would never make it, but they are going to have to watch you feast on the blessings and the breakthroughs of the Lord.

People may have said that you would never survive, but I'm telling you now that they can't believe where you are today. They talk about you, wondering what happened. Those haters have been sitting around munching on hater chips, drinking haterade, and eating hater tots. But don't you worry about all the folks who aren't rooting for you. Instead, look what the Lord has done for you!

I decided long ago that I wasn't going to let the haters get me. I made my haters my escalators. They can keep their hater chips because my God shall supply all my needs (Phil. 4:19). He has a plan for my life, and that plan is good. So I am going to feast at the table in the wilderness that the Lord has prepared for me. I am going to feast on His Word. I am going to dine in the presence of the Lord while my enemies keep eating those hater tots that are only going to hurt them, giving them heartburn, high blood pressure, and roots of bitterness rather than nourishing them, helping them, and healing them.

Remember this important fact: Your ultimate enemy is not a person or even a group of people. Your real enemy is not flesh and blood. Ephesians 6:12 says, "For we do not wrestle against flesh and blood, but against principalities, against powers, against the rulers of the darkness of this age, against spiritual hosts of wickedness in the heavenly places." The real battlefield is spiritual, not physical. We are not wrestling flesh and blood but the powers of darkness. The devil is the one I really want to watch me eat at the table in the wilderness.

You may be thinking that you don't deserve to feast with the Lord at His table. Well, listen to what the Word says:

> He brought me to the banqueting house, and his banner over me was love.
>
> —SONG OF SOLOMON 2:4

The devil is the one I really want to watch me eat at the table in the wilderness.

God doesn't bring you to the table, to His banquet, because you deserve it. He invites you to be in His presence, to dine with Him and feast on His Word, because He loves you! He loves you so much that He wants to announce it to the world. He loves you, and He wants to connect with you. So let me tell you this: It's time to eat. The Word of God is accessible to you today. It's time for you to feast on the Lord.

THE BREAD OF PRESENCE

You may feel like there are days when you can have the bread and some days when you can't have it. But that is not the case. The Bible says that the bread was set before the Lord continuously: "And you shall set the showbread on the table before Me always" (Exod. 25:30). Other translations use the terms "at all times," "continually," and "all the time" (AMP, NASB, NLV). It was always available. When you are sitting in church on Sunday, the bread is available. When you go out to lunch after church, the bread is still available. When you are chilling in your recliner on Sunday night after the kids go to bed, the bread is still available. On Monday mornings when you struggle to get your eyes open, the bread is still available. When people are talking about you, the bread is still available. When you fail, the bread is still available.

Now, the bread in the tabernacle wasn't just any bread. It was the bread of presence. In the Hebrew the word for bread, *lehem*, is immediately followed by the word *pānîm*. *Pānîm* means face, countenance, and presence. The showbread is the bread of God's presence. It's the face bread. The bread, as with everything else in the tabernacle, symbolizes God's desire to connect with you, His desire for you to spend time in His presence, face-to-face with Him.

There is nothing like being in the presence of the Lord. It changes you. When Moses spent time talking to the Lord face-to-face on Mount Sinai, it made the skin of his face shine. This wasn't a glow from being in the sun or a spray tan or even using some fancy moisturizer. It was a reflection of the glory of the Lord. And all the children of Israel could see it. Precious, when you are spending time in the presence of the Lord, people can tell. They can see it on your face. They can see it in your eyes. Being in the presence of the Lord changes you from the inside out, and everyone can see that.

The presence of the Lord also fills you all the way up with joy—and I mean real joy that is not based on your circumstances, joy that allows you to rejoice in the Lord even when your kids are crazy or your job is a joke or your money is funny. Psalm 16:11 says, "In Your presence is fullness of joy." I don't know about you, but I need fullness of joy in my life.

The presence of the Lord is also a source of rest, of peace. There isn't anywhere you can go that the presence of the Lord won't be. Psalm 139:7–10 says:

> Where can I go from Your Spirit? Or where can I flee from Your presence? If I ascend into heaven, You are there; if I make my bed in hell, behold, You are there. If I take the wings of the morning, and dwell in the uttermost parts of the sea, even there Your hand shall lead me, and Your right hand shall hold me.

No matter where you are, the presence of the Lord is there. He promised Moses, "My Presence will go with you, and I will give you rest" (Exod. 33:14), and the promise is for you too. God said, "I will never leave you nor forsake you" (Heb. 13:5). That is a promise you can count on.

Spending time in the presence of the Lord also equips and prepares you. Exodus 33:11 says, "So the LORD spoke to Moses face to face, as a man speaks to his friend. And he would return to the camp, but his servant Joshua the son of Nun, a young man, did not depart from the tabernacle."

As the leader of the children of Israel, Moses spent time in the presence of the Lord, and it equipped and prepared him for his role. But notice that even after Moses left the tabernacle, Joshua stayed put. He spent extra time hanging out with the Lord, and God raised him up to lead Israel after the death of Moses. The time Joshua spent in the presence of the Lord was preparing him to fulfill his purpose, just as spending time in the presence of the Lord prepares you to fulfill your purpose.

TIME TO DANCE

Second Timothy 1:9 says God "has saved us and called us with a holy calling, not according to our works, but according to His own purpose and grace which was given to us in Christ Jesus before time began." That means each of us has our own calling, our own purpose, specifically given to us before time began. There is something interesting about that verse in the Greek. The Greek word for purpose is *prothesis*. It means purpose or the setting forth of something. But the word also means showbread.[1]

If you're like me, you are thinking, "What in the world does showbread have to do with purpose?" We already talked about how spending time in the presence of the Lord equips and prepares you to fulfill your purpose, but let's dig a little deeper.

Second Corinthians 9:10 says, "Now may He who supplies seed to the sower, and bread for food, supply and multiply the seed you have sown and increase the fruits of your righteousness." The Greek word translated "supply" is *chorēgeō*.[2] It's where we get words like *choreograph* and *choreography*. Choreography refers to predetermined and assigned dance steps.

That means when God supplies your seed, He does so with predetermined plans for it. He says, "I give it to you having already predetermined what you should do with it." You are supposed to use some of it to live and some of it to sow. In other words, your seed comes to you on assignment! You have an assignment, a purpose, a plan, and your money does too. Your seed has an assignment, so if you eat your seed, you feed your need, but when you sow your seed, the Lord will multiply it. "He who sows sparingly will also reap sparingly, and he who sows bountifully will also reap bountifully" (2 Cor. 9:6).

The Greek word chorēgeō is also in 1 Peter 4:11, translated "supplies":

> If anyone ministers, let him do it as with the ability which God supplies, that in all things God may be glorified through Jesus Christ, to whom belong the glory and the dominion forever and ever.

While the Greek word does mean to give, supply, furnish, or minister, it literally means to be a dance leader, to lead someone in a dance.[3] Picture it like this: God has given you all kinds of talents and abilities. He gave you those gifts as a way to fulfill the holy calling on your life, your purpose. They are good gifts, and you can use them on your own and do some good things. It's like if you are naturally a good dancer, whenever you dance, it will be good. However, a naturally good dancer who has the chance to dance with the best dancer in the whole world is going to have their dancing taken to a whole other level—if the best dancer is allowed to lead. It won't just be good; it will be on a level you never could have imagined.

When it comes to gifts, talents, and abilities, the best dancer is the Lord. Let's face it: He created and purposefully designed all the gifts He gave you. There is no one who knows better how to use them to fulfill your purpose in the earth. So let God lead in how you use the gifts He has given you. He will take you to a whole other level.

I know right now you are probably thinking, "That's great, but I still don't know what that has to do with showbread." Well, in the Talmud, which contains teachings from ancient rabbis on the Law and theology, one of the rabbis said the showbread looked "like a dancing ship,"[4] or a dancing vessel. And that is exactly our purpose—to be vessels used by the Lord to fulfill His plans and purposes in the earth, and to allow the Lord to lead us in the dance as we minister "with the ability which God supplies." It is time to dance.

There is one other thing about the showbread that we can tie to purpose. The showbread was prepared for each Sabbath. That means there was fresh bread every week. While it is true that we each have an overarching purpose for our lives—to glorify the Lord and enjoy being in relationship with Him—we have other smaller purposes within our lives. From season to season and year to year those purposes can change. They can even change from week to week or day to day. So just like the priests had fresh showbread in the tabernacle each week, you can have fresh purpose each week. Ask the Lord each week, "What is Your purpose for me this week? What do You want me to do? What is my assignment?" Let Him lead you in the dance.

LET'S EAT!

There were twelve loaves of showbread baked every week for the tabernacle. They were placed in two rows of six on the table, and frankincense was put on each row "that it may be on the bread for a memorial, an offering made by fire to the LORD" (Lev. 24:6–7). When the priests replaced the showbread each week, they would eat the bread from the previous week. The loaves were specially made so they wouldn't get stale or moldy during the week. Only the priests were allowed to eat the showbread, and the Lord specifically said, "They shall eat it in a holy place; for it is most holy to him from the offerings of the LORD made by fire, by a perpetual statute" (Lev. 24:9).

Does that mean you aren't supposed to feast on the presence

and the Word of the Lord since it was meant only for the priests and only to be eaten in a holy place? No way! For the Word says, "You are a chosen generation, a royal priesthood, a holy nation, His own special people, that you may proclaim the praises of Him who called you out of darkness into His marvelous light" (1 Pet. 2:9). When you gave your life to Jesus, you became part of the royal priesthood of the one true God. Revelation 1:6 says that Jesus "has made us kings and priests to His God and Father."

The Word also says that "your body is the temple of the Holy Spirit" (1 Cor. 6:19). That means you are a walking, talking holy place. So let's eat! It's time to feast on the presence of the Lord and His Word! Remember, there is nothing more important in your life than the bread of God's presence and the bread of God's Word.

PRAYER

Lord, let Your Word guide me. Let Your presence guide me. God, I'm going to feast on Your Word. I'm going to feast on Your presence. And because of that, no weapon formed against me will prosper. Lord, help me to make spending time in Your presence and in Your Word a priority in my life. I declare that I'm going to hear Your Word and obey Your Word.

Lord, let Your presence change me. I want to be more like You. I want people to look at me and see a reflection of Your glory because of the time I spend with You. I want the fullness of joy, peace, and rest that come with Your presence. Let Your presence prepare me and equip me for Your purposes for my life. Lord, I will let You lead the dance. I declare that I will use the gifts You have given me and the seed You have given me according to Your predetermined plans. I won't keep everything for myself. I will sow bountifully so that I may reap bountifully.

I declare that I am part of Your royal priesthood and the temple of the Holy Spirit. I will feast on Your presence and on Your Word, and I will be forever changed. Thank You, Jesus, for Your presence and for Your Word. Amen.

JimRaleyBooks.com/chp7

Chapter 8

THE ALTAR OF INCENSE

God is Spirit, and those who worship Him
must worship in spirit and truth.
—JOHN 4:24

AFTER THE TABLE of showbread, the next place the priest would go was another altar. It was the last stop before going behind the veil, the last stop before entering the realm of no explanation. It was called the altar of worship, the altar of intercession, the altar of incense. The altar of incense was a beautiful place. The smoke that rose from the altar was a sweet-smelling fragrance to God, and it represented worship.

If I'm going to make it, I need to be a worshipper. You need to be a worshipper. We all need to be worshippers. You see, miracles open up for worshippers. The mercy seat opens up for worshippers. Another level opens up for worshippers. A new dimension opens up for worshippers. The realm of no explanation opens up for worshippers.

There is a difference between being a worshipper and being religious. Don't be religious; be a worshipper. People who are religious go through the motions of worship without any heart behind it. That is not what God wants. He wants true worshippers.

> But the hour is coming, and now is, when the true wor-shipers will worship the Father in spirit and truth; for the Father is seeking such to worship Him. God is Spirit, and those who worship Him must worship in spirit and truth.
> —John 4:23–24

God is looking for people who will worship Him in spirit and in truth, not out of tradition, habit, obligation, or duty. We worship Him because He loves us. We worship Him because of all He has done for us, especially because of the finished work of Jesus on the cross. We worship Him because of who He is. He is forever worthy of our praise. Amen!

The Fire of Worship

The incense was placed on the altar to be burned by the priest. In order for something to be burned, it needs fire. The fire used to light the incense came from the brazen altar. Remember, it was the Lord Himself who sent the fire that consumed the first burnt offering on the brazen altar:

> Then Aaron lifted his hand toward the people, blessed them, and came down from offering the sin offering, the burnt offering, and peace offerings. And Moses and Aaron went into the tabernacle of meeting, and came

out and blessed the people. Then the glory of the LORD appeared to all the people, and fire came out from before the LORD and consumed the burnt offering and the fat on the altar. When all the people saw it, they shouted and fell on their faces.

—LEVITICUS 9:22–24

The glory of the Lord came down in the holy of holies and hit the mercy seat, and the fire went underneath the curtain, underneath the veil, and out into the outer court, all the way to the altar. And that is the fire we need. Let me tell you, I want supernatural fire. I don't want a fire that a man lights. I don't want a fire that a man produces. I need fire out of the glory. I need fire out of the presence of God. I need fire out of the realm of no explanation.

> *God is looking for people who will worship Him in spirit and in truth, not out of tradition, habit, obligation, or duty.*

The Lord instructed that the fire on the altar must be kept burning continuously. It was so important that He said it three times in a row (Lev. 6:9, 12, 13). Because the fire on the brazen altar was never allowed to go out, the fire used on the altar of incense came from God Himself. Don't miss this. The fire that had come from the Lord provided the fire for worship on the altar of incense. In other words, the worship came because of what had happened at the altar.

Too often our worship comes because the music is good. Too often our experience comes because we like the singer or we like the song or we like the atmosphere. No; God said, "If you're going to worship Me, you need to go all the way back to the altar, all the way back to the cross, all the way back to the blood, all the way back to the sacrifice of Jesus, all the way back to your salvation—that's when you can bring Me real worship. You can't bring Me worship until you remember what Jesus did for you."

Have you ever watched someone and thought, "She is a worshipper"? Have you ever noticed someone whose worship made you think, "He is a worshipper"? Then one day you see them and they just look miserable in church. You wonder, "What happened to them?" I'll tell you what happened to them. They forgot the cross, they forgot the blood, and they forgot how they were changed at the altar.

The altar, the place of sacrifice, is the source of the fire that causes true worship to arise from the altar of incense. You can't forget the source. You can't forget the goodness of God. You can't forget all that He has done to connect with you. You can't forget all the miracles you have experienced, all the unexplainable things God did in your life. I declare you're not going to forget the goodness of the Lord in your life, and you're going to worship Him from a place of redemption.

The altar, the place of sacrifice, is the source of the fire that causes true worship to arise from the altar of incense. You can't forget the source. You can't forget the goodness of God.

The incense was also a symbol of intercession. Remember the sons of Korah we talked about earlier? Korah was the instigator of a rebellion against Moses, and it did not end well for him.

Now it came to pass, as [Moses] finished speaking all these words, that the ground split apart under [Korah and the other leaders of the rebellion], and the earth opened its mouth and swallowed them up, with their households and all the men with Korah, with all their goods. So they and all those with them went down alive into the pit; the earth closed over them, and they perished from among the assembly.

—Numbers 16:31–33

Then the other 250 men who also rebelled were consumed by fire that came out from the Lord. You would think the children of Israel would have seen that going against Moses, whom God had clearly chosen and anointed to lead them, was not such a great idea. But this is the children of Israel we're talking about, and they didn't always make the best choices. They "complained against Moses and Aaron, saying, 'You have killed the people of the Lord'" (Num. 16:41). As soon as they complained, the glory of the Lord appeared at the tabernacle, and it wasn't going to end well for the children of Israel either. A plague had begun. But Moses knew what to do.

So Moses said to Aaron, "Take a censer and put fire in it from the altar, put incense on it, and take it quickly to the congregation and make atonement for them; for wrath has gone out from the Lord. The plague has begun." Then Aaron took it as Moses commanded, and ran into the midst of the assembly; and already the plague had begun among the people. So he put in the incense and made atonement for the people. And he stood between the dead and the living; so the plague was stopped.

—Numbers 16:46–48

Moses told Aaron to get a censer and run around with it to intercede for the people and make atonement for them. Everywhere Aaron went with the censer of incense, the plague was lifted. The incense represents intercession.

I'm declaring that when you pray, when you seek the face of God, your prayers will rise like the fragrance of the burning incense before the Lord. Your prayers of intercession will be lifted before the throne of heaven. The intercession is going to break the attack on your children. It's going to break the attack on your family. It is going to break any attacks of the enemy in your life. Hallelujah!

YOU HAVE TO MAKE IT

The golden altar was called the altar of incense, the altar of worship, or the altar of intercession. It represents so many things, but the strongest picture of this altar is that it is a place of worship and prayer.

Worship is intentional. It's not accidental. You make a place for God. You make a place for worship.

Exodus 30:1 says, "You shall make an altar to burn incense on." Hear me now: When you make an altar, it will make you. When you make an altar of worship and prepare an altar of worship, that place of worship will make you. It will change you. It will transform you.

The verse in Exodus came alive to me because it says you have to *make* it. You have to make this altar of worship. *Make* means to be intentional in what you do. It means to prepare, to build, to create. Do you know what that tells me? It tells me that worship is intentional. It's not accidental. You make a place for God. You make a place for worship. Prayer is also intentional. It's something you create space for. It's when you say, "Lord, this is for You. This moment, this time, is for You." Make it a point to create space for prayer and worship in your life.

To *make* means to create or to build. The Hebrew word for make, *'āśâ*, is very powerful. It literally means to do or to make. But it also means to press or to squeeze.[1] There are times when life is going to be tough. There are times when life will be so intense and situations will be so overwhelming that you won't feel like worshipping. There will be times when you won't feel like praying. There will be times when you won't feel like exalting the Lord and praising His name. There will be times when your feelings get the better of you and you won't feel like glorifying the Lord. But those times when you don't feel like praising are the moments when you need to make yourself give Him praise.

It is in those times that you need to make an altar of worship. It's in those moments when you must command your soul to bless the mighty name of the Lord. That's when you squeeze yourself, press yourself, and make yourself worship and praise. That is when you say, "Lord, even though things are not perfect, even though things are not the way I want them to be, I'm going to open up my mouth and give You a mighty praise anyhow." That anyhow worship—when you are being squeezed and pressed but you choose to squeeze and press out worship anyhow—is powerful.

Have you ever brought God anyhow worship? Things are not going well, but you worship Him anyhow. Your marriage is struggling, but you worship Him anyhow. Things are not perfect, but you worship Him anyhow. In that moment you understand 1 Thessalonians 5:18: "In everything give thanks;

for this is the will of God in Christ Jesus for you." It's when you press and you squeeze and you say, "God, I'm not going to let my moment become my misery. I'm going to worship You. I'm going to magnify You." You choose to make an altar of worship in your life.

FIRE, BLOOD, AND POWER

As with all the other furniture in the tabernacle, the Lord gave Moses specific instructions about the altar of incense:

> You shall make an altar to burn incense on; you shall make it of acacia wood. A cubit shall be its length and a cubit its width—it shall be square—and two cubits shall be its height. Its horns shall be of one piece with it. And you shall overlay its top, its sides all around, and its horns with pure gold; and you shall make for it a molding of gold all around. Two gold rings you shall make for it, under the molding on both its sides. You shall place them on its two sides, and they will be holders for the poles with which to bear it. You shall make the poles of acacia wood, and overlay them with gold. And you shall put it before the veil that is before the ark of the Testimony, before the mercy seat that is over the Testimony, where I will meet with you. Aaron shall burn on it sweet incense every morning; when he tends the lamps, he shall burn incense on it. And when Aaron lights the lamps at twilight, he shall burn incense on it, a perpetual incense before the LORD throughout your generations. You shall not offer strange incense on it, or a burnt offering, or a grain offering; nor shall you pour a drink offering on it. And Aaron shall make atonement upon its horns once a year with the blood of the sin offering of atonement;

once a year he shall make atonement upon it throughout your generations. It is most holy to the LORD.

—EXODUS 30:1–10

The altar was about a foot and a half long and wide, and it was about three feet tall. It had a horn on each corner. It was overlaid with gold and had a gold molding, like a crown, all the way around.

When the priest came to the altar of incense, he did two things that were significant. He anointed the horns with blood, and he brought fire from the brazen altar to the altar of worship. God was very clear in Exodus 30 about what to do and what not to do. But there were two priests, Nadab and Abihu, who offered "strange fire" on the altar of incense (Lev. 10:1, KJV), and they were killed for it, consumed by fire from the Lord. Why was it "strange fire"? It was strange fire because it did not come off the altar of sacrifice, the brazen altar. It was worship that had not been covered in the blood. They had convinced themselves that it didn't matter where the fire came from. Any fire would do. God wouldn't care.

The truth is the fire that lit the incense rose as a sweet-smelling savor or fragrance to God. God loved the smell of that worship—but it had to come from the right source. It had to be the right fire from the right altar. Nadab and Abihu got their fire from another source; that was the problem. Their worship wasn't covered in the blood.

Nadab and Abihu needed fire covered by the blood of the sin offering made on the brazen altar. Our sin offering was made by Jesus on the cross. For us, the brazen altar represents the cross of Jesus Christ. It represents the blood of Jesus Christ. We bring worship that is cross filtered, worship offered in response to what Jesus has done for us. We worship Him because of the blood. We worship because we are redeemed. We worship because we have been saved and set free from the wages of sin. We worship because He has been so good to us in providing His only Son as the sin offering we needed in order to have unbroken fellowship with Him, to be connected to Him.

All of our worship must be cross filtered. It doesn't matter how good it sounds. It doesn't matter how polished the worship is. It doesn't matter how professional or skilled the singers and musicians are. If the fire of worship does not have the altar, or the cross, as its source, it's strange to God. That's why we can't just gather with professional musicians. We can't just sound good. Our worship has to come from a place of thankfulness because God has redeemed us. We've been forgiven, saved, sanctified, and set free because we've been to the cross, because we are covered by the blood of Jesus—and that's why we worship.

If you can't praise God for anything else, you can praise Him because you've been to the cross and you've been covered by the blood. The New King James Version uses the word *profane* to describe fire that doesn't come from the brazen altar. God says, "If you're worshipping Me just because the music sounds good, that's strange to Me. If you're worshipping just because you're grooving to the beat, that's strange to Me." That's strange fire. But if you come into a service and they begin to sing "Miracle Mercy," and you remember where you used to be and where you are now, and you lift your hands and begin to glorify God, He says, "I love that; keep it coming."

The altar of worship had four horns. Remember, the

tabernacle is full of types and shadows. Horns in the Bible represent the power of an animal. So when you come to the altar of worship and see the horns, it's a reminder of where real power is found.

Real power is not found in your gift. Real power is not found in your money. Real power is not found in your skill. Real power is not found in your ability. Real power is found when you open up your mouth and begin to glorify God. Real power is when you say, "I'm not great, Lord, but You are. I'm not powerful, God, but You are. I can't do it, but You can. I can't shift it, but You can." It's when you acknowledge the greatness of the One who is able to do exceedingly abundantly above all that you could ask or imagine. It's when you recognize that the God of the unexplainable is worthy of all your praise.

> **Real power is not found in your gift, your money, or your skill. Real power is found when you open up your mouth and begin to glorify God.**

Horns in the Bible represent strength; they represent power. Have you ever been weak and felt like you'd gone as far as you could go, but then you enter a place where you worship God and His strength is made perfect in your weakness? When you choose to worship God, even when you are at the end of your rope, you acknowledge where true power and strength come from.

Horns were also used for something else—anointing. The Israelites would hollow out the horns and fill them with oil to anoint priests and kings. When the Lord sent the prophet Samuel to anoint David king, He told him, "Fill your horn with oil....I will show you what you shall do; you shall anoint for Me the one I name to you" (1 Sam. 16:1, 3). David was anointed king with a horn of oil.

Worship doesn't just bring power—it brings anointing. Power and anointing are found in worship. Do you want to find people who really know what it is to flow in power, signs, miracles, and wonders, with the unexplainable manifesting in their lives? They are the ones who know how to worship the Lord. When you worship the Lord, when you acknowledge His greatness, you find power and anointing. Worship brings the power to walk in freedom. It brings anointing to break the yoke. It brings anointing to lift burdens. Hallelujah!

CHASE THE SNAKES AWAY

The Lord also gave Moses specific instructions about the incense for the tabernacle:

> Take sweet spices, stacte and onycha and galbanum, and pure frankincense with these sweet spices; there shall be equal amounts of each. You shall make of these an incense, a compound according to the art of the perfumer, salted, pure, and holy. And you shall beat some of it very fine, and put some of it before the Testimony in the tabernacle of meeting where I will meet with you. It shall be most holy to you. But as for the incense which you shall make, you shall not make any for yourselves, according to its composition. It shall be to you holy for the LORD.
>
> —EXODUS 30:34–37

So the four main ingredients—stacte, onycha, galbanum, and pure frankincense—were mixed together with salt. The Bible says all these ingredients had to be beaten fine. They went through the process to be beaten fine, and in the beating, they became more valuable to God. He could use them. The process set them apart to be used for God.

The devil thinks that when we face seasons when we're enduring a beating and it feels like we've been beaten fine, he's going to get the last laugh; he thinks he is going to destroy our lives. But I'm here to tell you that sometimes the worship you bring God is wounded worship. Sometimes things are not perfect, but you say, "God, I am hurting, but I'm not going to stop worshipping. I am struggling, but I'm not going to stop worshipping. I'm persevering, and I'm still praising. I'm weak, but I'm still giving You glory."

I won't stop worshipping, no matter what the season I'm in looks like. No matter what happens, even when I'm taking a beating from life, I'm not going to shut my mouth. I am going to open my mouth and give the Lord a mighty praise, no matter what my circumstances are. I have made up my mind. I have decided that I'm going to be a worshipper. I'm not going to let my worship be limited by the amount of money I have in the bank. I'm not going to let my worship be stopped by my family going crazy. I'm not going to be silent instead of worshipping just because some haters are talking bad about me. I'm not going to let my worship be silenced by the fact that everything isn't going perfectly. I will open up my mouth and give God glory no matter what season I'm in because I know that He is greater than I am.

You may be thinking, "I can't worship the Lord because I've got too many blemishes in my past," or "I've been struggling, so I can't worship the Lord," or "I can't worship because I feel unworthy." Well, let me ring hell's bells. Let me give you a word that will shift your life: You don't worship God because you're worthy; you worship the Lord because He's worthy. You worship the Lord because He is good, not because you're good.

I've taught about the tabernacle for years. It's one of my favorite things to teach. But I heard something just recently that thrilled me deep down in my heart. The stacte, onycha, galbanum, frankincense, and salt were stirred together and then poured over this altar, where they caught on fire. The smoke that rose filled up the tent, but it was so strong that it permeated the tent. Jewish oral tradition (the Mishnah) says that during the days of the temple in Jerusalem, the fragrance of the incense could be smelled all the way in Jericho, about twelve miles away.[2]

That means during the days of the tabernacle, the fragrance of the incense would have gone outside the tent and into the camp. The aroma got into people's homes. The aroma was present in their family gatherings. It was there at the dinner table. It was there when they were working, doing chores, and playing with their children. The fragrance of worship permeated their lives.

That is what I want in my life. I want the fragrance of worship everywhere I go, not just in a church building. I want it in my home, at my dinner table, in my car. The fragrance of worship smells good to God, but it also smells good to people.

There's another powerful truth about the fragrance of the incense—it chased the snakes away. The scent of galbanum, specifically, repels snakes. In the camp of the children of Israel, the fragrance of the incense of worship physically chased the snakes away. But the fragrance of worship chases other snakes away too. It's time to open your mouth and let your worship chase away the snakes in your life. Chase depression away. Chase thoughts of suicide away. Chase fear away. Chase the lies of the enemy away. Chase lust away. Chase envy away. Chase anxiety away.

What are you waiting for? Demons and devils run when you start worshipping God. Satan's strongholds break when you worship the Lord. If you want to chase the snakes away, open up your mouth and worship.

Check out one more detail about the incense: It was for the Lord only. This is powerful. The incense smelled wonderful, and it changed the camp. But God said, "Don't make it for yourself." The incense was holy for the Lord. It was for His glory, and for His alone. Using the incense intended to worship the Lord for your own self-gratification, for your own flesh, was a big no-no. Worship is meant for the Lord only.

The truth of the matter is that men can't handle worship. Anytime people start being worshipped, they self-destruct. They commit suicide. They fail in their ministries. They fail in their opportunities because they receive worship unto themselves. God said, "If you do that, I will cut you off." (See Exodus 30:38.) Receiving worship unto yourself is an easy trap for preachers to fall into, but we need to remember who really deserves the glory, who really deserves the worship.

I've been a preacher for thirty-something years. I've never saved anybody. I've never redeemed anybody. I've never healed anybody. I've never set anybody free. But I have glorified the One who is able to do exceedingly abundantly above everything I can ask because I cannot afford to be cut off. I can't make it without His presence. I cannot be cut off. Worship belongs to God alone. It's not us; it's Him.

The altar of worship was the last stop before the priest entered the holy of holies. It was the final stop before entering the miracle zone, the realm of no explanation. Are you ready to enter the miracle zone? Then make an altar of worship, give all the glory to the Lord for the great things He has done, and get ready.

PRAYER

Lord, I choose to make an altar of worship. I choose to worship You because You alone are worthy of all my praise. I will not forget Your goodness. I will not forget the way You redeemed me, saved me, and set me free by the blood of Jesus Christ. Thank You, Lord! Even when I am feeling beaten, I will choose to worship You anyhow. No matter the circumstances in my life, You are worthy. You are wonderful, and I open my mouth to give You a mighty praise!

In the mighty name of Jesus, I pray that when I open my mouth to worship the Lord, all the snakes in my life will be chased away. Fear will leave. Depression and anxiety will leave. Your strength is made perfect in my weakness. I magnify and glorify Your holy name, Jesus! Let my worship arise before You as a sweet-smelling fragrance, and let that fragrance permeate my whole life.

JimRaleyBooks.com/chp8

Chapter 9

THE VEIL

Then, behold, the veil of the temple was
torn in two from top to bottom.
—Matthew 27:51

THE GATE TO the tabernacle looked different to set it apart as the entrance. The screen on the five pillars looked different from the rest of the walls surrounding the holy place, again marking it as the entrance. And as the priest proceeded through the tabernacle, there was one more entrance—the veil. The veil marked the entrance to the holy of holies, the most holy place, the place of God's manifest presence, the place of mercy, the place of miracles—the realm of no explanation.

FROM TOP TO BOTTOM

As with everything else in the tabernacle, the Lord gave Moses specific instructions about the veil separating the holy of holies from the rest of the tabernacle:

> You shall make a veil woven of blue, purple, and scarlet thread, and fine woven linen. It shall be woven with an artistic design of cherubim. You shall hang it upon the four pillars of acacia wood overlaid with gold. Their hooks shall be gold, upon four sockets of silver. And you shall hang the veil from the clasps. Then you shall bring the ark of the Testimony in there, behind the veil. The veil shall be a divider for you between the holy place and the Most Holy.
>
> —Exodus 26:31–33

The screen marking the entrance to the holy place, you remember, was on five pillars. In my opinion, those five pillars represent the facets of the character of God revealed in Isaiah 9:6: "Wonderful, Counselor, Mighty God, Everlasting Father, Prince of Peace."

The veil marking the entrance to the holy of holies was on four pillars. The number four is found many times in the Bible. There were four rivers in the Garden of Eden, there were four living creatures around the throne of God in John's vision of heaven in Revelation, there are several references to the four winds, etc. But these four posts mark the entrance to the presence of God. When you spend time in the presence of God, you get to know Him in a personal way. You get to understand His character, who He is, how He operates. And when I think of the number four in connection with getting to know the Lord and who He really is, I think of the four Gospels: Matthew, Mark, Luke, and John.

Just as the veil was a doorway, the Gospels are a doorway. They are an opening for you to get to know God, to spend time in His presence, to learn about His character, to discover who He really is and how He wants to work in your life. The Gospels are the good news of Jesus Christ.

The whole tabernacle points to Jesus and the salvation He was going to provide on the cross at Calvary. Jesus is the foundation. He is the way in. Remember, a relationship with the Lord is vital if you want to enter the realm of no explanation, if you want to see His miracles manifesting in your life. Do you really want to know the Lord? Then get to know Him by reading the Gospels, the account of God in human flesh walking the earth, teaching the truth, healing the sick and the broken, paying the price for our salvation, and setting us free.

I am so grateful for the gospel, the Word of God. I am so grateful for the good news. And I am so grateful for what the Gospels of Matthew, Mark, Luke, and John tell us happened to the veil at the entrance to the holy of holies.

You see, eventually the tabernacle was replaced by the temple in Jerusalem. The tabernacle was needed while the children of Israel were wandering in the wilderness, but after they arrived in the Promised Land, a permanent dwelling place for the presence of the Lord could be built. Even the fact that God initially had the children of Israel build a mobile dwelling place for His presence speaks of His desire to connect with His people. While they were wandering in the wilderness, He wanted to make sure they knew His presence was with them wherever they went.

When the temple was built, just like in the tabernacle, the

veil marked the entrance to the holy of holies and separated it from the rest of temple. Normally when we hear the word *veil*, we often think of a bride's veil, a light, sheer piece of fabric that can be easily torn. But the veil in the tabernacle and the temple was not that kind of veil. It was a very heavy, thick curtain.

In the tabernacle, the veil was ten cubits tall by twelve cubits wide, or about fifteen feet by eighteen feet. In the temple during the time of the Gospels, the veil was twenty cubits by forty cubits, or about thirty feet by sixty feet.

While the Bible doesn't tell us the thickness of the veil, we know from multiple sources that it was very thick. The Mishnah tells us that the veil was woven from seventy-two strands of yarn, with each strand made of twenty-four threads, and the thickness was equal to the width of a man's hand, or about four inches. It was so heavy that when it needed to be cleaned, it took three hundred priests to carry it.[1] This was no flimsy bridal veil.

The veil physically separating the people from the presence of God was heavy, just as the weight of the sin that separates us from God is heavy. The veil separated an uncommon God from common men. But remember, God wants to connect with us. He wants to enjoy being in relationship with us. He wants us to enjoy being in His presence.

Separation was not what He wanted, but because He is a holy God, when sin entered the picture, it did separate us from Him. Because He is holy, our sin was a barrier to His presence. But God didn't want that barrier to remain, which is why from the moment when Adam and Eve sinned in the Garden of Eden, He had a plan to remove the separation, to remove the barrier of sin. He told the serpent, "And I will put enmity between you and the woman, and between your seed and her Seed; He shall bruise your head, and you shall bruise His heel" (Gen. 3:15). God was planning all along to send Jesus as a sacrifice, the perfect sacrifice to atone for our sins once and for all. Yes, Satan would get a lick in on Jesus, bruising His heel, but Jesus would win the battle, bruising Satan's head and taking him out.

The moment Jesus died on the cross at Calvary, bearing the weight of the sins of the world, the battle was won. Satan may not have realized it, but it was over. Jesus said, "It is finished!" (John 19:30), and it was. And at that moment, when Jesus willingly died for you and me and for everyone else who would believe in Him, "the veil of the temple was torn in two from top to bottom" (Matt. 27:51). The barrier was removed, once and for all. As John 3:16 says, "For God so loved the world that He gave His only begotten Son, that whoever believes in Him should not perish but have everlasting life." God made a way for us to be with Him and enjoy His presence for all eternity.

Don't miss that the veil was torn from top to bottom. If it had been torn from bottom to top, it could have been done by men. But the Bible said when Jesus died on the cross, the veil was torn from the top to the bottom. It was like God said, "No more separation. I have come now to My people through Jesus. I made a way for My children to be in My presence forever."

There is no more separation, no more division. Anyone who chooses to believe in the mighty name of Jesus and accept His forgiveness for their sins has free and open access to the presence of God. The veil is no longer a barrier, nor are the sins that have been washed away by the cleansing blood of Jesus. Jesus paid the price to give us uninhibited access to the presence of God, and the veil being torn from top to bottom declared that loud and clear.

BEHIND THE VEIL

Behind the veil was the most special place in the tabernacle: the holy of holies. It was the place where the presence of God was. It was the place where the ark of the covenant was kept. It was the place of mercy. It was the realm of no explanation. It was the place of miracles.

The holy of holies was the realm of the supernatural, the realm of no explanation.

Behind the veil was where the glory of the Lord manifested. Remember that in the outer court was natural light that allowed you to see what was going on. In the inner court was candlelight from the golden lampstand that allowed you to see. But the holy of holies was different. The light didn't come from the sun or from a candlestick. The light came from the manifest glory of the Lord God Almighty. The holy of holies was the realm of the supernatural, the realm of no explanation.

When you are in the presence of the Lord, when you see His glory manifesting in your life, you can't explain the goings on. You can't explain what's happening. You just know you're in the presence of God and the supernatural is taking place. You transcend the natural realm where you depend on man to bring you breakthroughs and man to bring you oil and man to give you the job and man to make it right. You go behind the veil and enter a season of supernatural breakthrough. You can't explain how your children finally got saved. You don't have an explanation for how the cancer disappeared. You don't know how the money came in. You don't know how you got set free from that addiction. You don't know how you got that job. You can't explain how your marriage was restored. But you got into God's presence, and everything shifted.

The key is found in the process. You have to enter into the process of the Lord, the process of making your way into the presence of the Lord that is reflected in the tabernacle.

The priest approached the tabernacle, carrying the weight of everything he had been through. Every broken place that he walked through, every hard thing that he faced was all about getting here. He approached the gate with praise. He stopped at the altar of sacrifice, a place of atonement, a place of covenant and connection, a place of offering, a place of dying to the flesh. Then he went to the laver, a place to be washed by the water of the Word, a place to be cleansed from all unrighteousness, a place to come clean.

Then the priest approached the inner court, passing through the five pillars, reminding Him of the Lord, who is Wonderful, Counselor, Mighty God, Everlasting Father, and Prince of Peace. Then he was in the inner court, with the golden lampstand, the table of showbread, and the altar of incense, and all that they represented: the oil and fire of the Spirit, feasting on the presence of the Lord and pursuing His calling in our lives, and worshipping the Lord, who is worthy of all our praise. It was all part of the journey to what was behind the veil. It was all part of getting him to the glory.

All the things you have gone through are getting you to the glory. All the brokenness, all the heartache, all the struggles are getting you to the glory. When you open your mouth and give God a mighty praise, it's getting you to the glory. When you repent and allow your sins to be washed away by the blood of Jesus, it's getting you to the glory. When you die to your flesh, it's getting you to the glory.

When you passionately pursue your God-given purpose, when you allow God to lead you, when you worship Him with your whole heart, it's all getting you to the glory.

When you open up your Bible and let the water of the Word wash you clean, it's getting you to the glory. When you deepen your understanding of God's character and who He really is, it's getting you to the glory. When you are filled with the Holy Spirit, when you passionately pursue your God-given purpose, when you allow God to lead you, when you worship Him with your whole heart no matter what, it's all getting you to the glory. It's getting you behind the veil. It's getting you to the mercy seat. It's getting you to the place of miracles. It's getting you to the realm of no explanation.

PRAYER

Lord, the pillars of the veil remind me of who You are. In the Gospel of Matthew, You spoke to the storm and it stopped. So Lord, I declare that I will trust You to calm the storms that the enemy tries to bring against me. I raise my hands and tell the devil in advance that even if he brings a storm against me, I have the Prince of Peace onboard my boat, and everything is going to be just fine. Lord, I read in Mark that You healed the woman with the issue of blood. So I declare that every issue that I have will be healed by You. You are taking care of my issues, God—my financial issues, my health issues, my anger issues, my unforgiveness issues, my past issues, my present issues, my future issues.

Lord, in Luke, I read that You healed the multitudes. So I thank You for the mighty revival of healing that's going to come. It's going to be released in my family and in my church. Lord, in John 3:16, I read that You said You were salvation for the whole world. I declare that people are coming to the kingdom. I declare that my lost loved ones will be saved this year. I speak in faith. I'm praying for all the sons and daughters of God to be set free this year. I declare that my lost loved ones will know that "God so loved the world that He gave His only begotten son, that whosoever believes in Him should not perish."

Lord, I thank You that when You died on the cross, the veil separating me from You was torn from top to bottom. Lord, I thank You that there is nothing separating me from You because of the work of Jesus on the cross. I thank You that my sins are covered in the blood so that I can boldly enter Your presence.

Lord, I am ready to go behind the veil. I am ready for Your glory to manifest in my life. I am ready to run to the mercy seat. I am ready for the realm of no explanation, the realm of miracles. Thank You, Jesus!

JimRaleyBooks.com/chp9

Chapter 10

THE ARK OF THE COVENANT

*But you are a chosen generation, a royal priesthood, a
holy nation, His own special people, that you may proclaim the praises of Him who called you out of darkness into His marvelous light; who once were not a
people but are now the people of God, who had not
obtained mercy but now have obtained mercy.*
—1 PETER 2:9–10

WHEN THE PRIEST walked behind the veil, he was in the
presence of the Lord. The holy of holies was the location of the manifest presence of the Lord on the earth. It was
the place where heaven came to earth. The holy of holies,
the realm of no explanation, is the final destination in the
journey through the tabernacle.

Remember, there was no light source inside the holy of
holies—other than the glory of the Lord. There was no

sunlight like in the outer court. There was no lamplight like in the inner court, or holy place. There was just the glory. Do you know what that tells me? No matter how dark your circumstances, no matter how deep the hole you have dug for yourself, no matter how dim your outlook, no matter how dismal your life seems, the glory of the Lord can light it up!

No matter how dark your circumstances, no matter how dismal your life seems, the glory of the Lord can light it up!

The Word says, "In [Jesus] was life, and the life was the light of mankind. The light shines in darkness, but the darkness has not overcome it" (John 1:4–5, MEV). That means there is no darkness so dark or deep that the light and love and glory of the King of kings and Lord of lords can't light it up. Light always overcomes the dark.

Beyond the veil, inside the holy of holies was just one piece of furniture: the ark of the covenant, or the ark of the testimony. The mercy seat rested on top of the ark of the covenant. The Lord told Moses how to make the ark:

> And they shall make an ark of acacia wood; two and a half cubits shall be its length, a cubit and a half its width, and a cubit and a half its height. And you shall overlay it with pure gold, inside and out you shall overlay it, and shall make on it a molding of gold all around. You shall cast four rings of gold for it, and put them in its four corners; two rings shall be on one side, and two rings on the other side. And you shall make poles of acacia wood, and overlay them with gold. You shall put the poles into the rings on the sides of the ark, that the ark may be carried by them. The poles shall be in the rings of the

ark; they shall not be taken from it. And you shall put
into the ark the Testimony which I will give you.

—EXODUS 25:10–16

The ark of the covenant represents the throne of God on the earth. The Bible says that it is overlaid with gold, inside and out. The gold represents God's goodness and mercy. God is good inside and out. God is always good. He is always worthy.

The ark had four corners, each with a gold ring, so there were four gold rings. We've already talked about how the number four points us toward the Gospels. The Gospels of Jesus Christ—Matthew, Mark, Luke, and John—recall the goodness of God's mercy and grace through the manifestation of Jesus:

> And the Word became flesh and dwelt among us, and we beheld His glory, the glory as of the only begotten of the Father, full of grace and truth....And of His fullness we have all received, and grace for grace. For the law was given through Moses, but grace and truth came through Jesus Christ...."For God so loved the world that He gave His only begotten Son, that whoever believes in Him should not perish but have everlasting life. For God did not send His Son into the world to condemn the world, but that the world through Him might be saved."
>
> —JOHN 1:14, 16–17; 3:16–17

The Gospels tell us that we come to mercy not because we deserve it but because of God's amazing grace. They tell us that we have everything we have not because we're so good or because we've got it going on, but instead because of the goodness of our great God.

The gospel, the good news of the saving and redeeming work of Jesus Christ, is what changes lives. It's the gospel that has the power to change us. The gospel changed my life. If you are a believer in Jesus Christ, the risen Son of God, the Lamb of God who takes away the sins of the world, then the gospel changed your life too. When you have Jesus, things change. Your life changes. You change.

I know I wouldn't be here without Jesus and His gospel. I know it's the gospel that has made me who I am. I know that it was Jesus who made me who I am. I know that it was the Savior, the Healer, the Redeemer, the Provider, the Ancient of Days. I know it was the One called Wonderful, Counselor, Mighty God, Everlasting Father, Prince of Peace. He is God Almighty, the God who sees, the Lord who sanctifies, the Lord our banner. He is the captain of the host of heaven, the living Word, our living hope, the Rock of our salvation. He is the Alpha and the Omega, the Beginning and the End. He is the way, the truth, and the life. He is Messiah. He is Immanuel, God with us. He is Jesus, and there is none like Him.

The four corners on the ark of the covenant also represent the four cardinal directions: north, south, east, and west. You know what that tells me? Because the mercy seat is right on top of the ark, there's nowhere mercy can't go. It doesn't matter how far you get away from God; mercy will run you down. It doesn't matter how lost people are; mercy will go where they are. Mercy will go from Alabama to Alaska, from Argentina to Austria, and from Australia to Africa. Mercy makes all the difference in the world, all over the world. It can go anywhere, from the back room to the boardroom to the classroom. It will go from God's house to the crack house to the White House. It will go from the front row to skid row to death row. Hallelujah!

IN THE ARK

Inside the ark, underneath the mercy seat, were three things: the two stone tablets with the Ten Commandments written on them, a golden jar of the manna the Lord provided for the children of Israel when they were wandering in the wilderness, and Aaron's rod that budded.

God gave the Ten Commandments to Moses knowing full well that humanity would struggle to keep them. He knew we could not flawlessly keep the Law. You can act religious if you want to, like you have it all together and you never sin. But the truth is all of us have sinned. All of us have struggled to keep even the most basic commandments.

You might say, "Well, I've never killed anybody," but the Word says, "Whoever hates his brother is a murderer" (1 John 3:15). You might say, "I've never committed adultery," but have you lusted after someone in your heart? Jesus said, "But I say to you that whoever looks at a woman to lust for her has already committed adultery with her in his heart" (Matt. 5:28). At one time or another we have all lied. We have all lusted. We have all envied. We have all hated. We have all said things we shouldn't. We have all let things in our hearts that shouldn't be there. None of us is perfect.

So the Lord put those commandments in the ark of the covenant to show you and me that we need another source, to show us that we cannot be flawless, cannot be perfect. But do you know what He did after He had Moses put the Ten Commandments in the ark? He put mercy over the top of them. He knew that we would struggle. He knew that we would fall. He knew that we would fail. He knew that we would miss the mark. He knew that we would cross the line.

161

Mercy was in His plan all along. I'm here today only because a loving God put mercy over the top of my failures. I praise Him for His abundant mercy that covers all my sin!

MIRACLE PROVISION

Next in the ark of the covenant was the golden jar of manna. It represents God's miracle mercy provision. It doesn't represent that the Israelites were perfect. It doesn't represent that they deserved God's provision. The manna was God's way of saying, "Even when you're losing your mind, even when you're doubting, even when you're turning your back on Me, even when you're not being who you ought to be, even when you forget Me, I won't forget you. I'll keep providing for you. I'll keep making a way for you. I'll keep bringing you manna in the morning. I'll keep opening doors for you until you realize that you didn't get there by yourself."

God's miracle mercy provision doesn't always look the way we expect it to look.

I can tell you right now, I'm where I am today only because of the miracle mercy manifestation of God's provision in my life. God was good to me even when I wasn't good to Him. God was faithful to me even when I wasn't faithful to Him. God provided even when I lost my mind and lost my way. Manna still fell from heaven in my life. I still had food on the table. I still had family that loved me. At the mercy seat we're reminded of God's faithfulness and provision even when we don't deserve it.

Here's one other thing to remember about the manna: God's miracle mercy provision doesn't always look the way we expect it to look. When the children of Israel were wandering in the wilderness and God first provided them manna for food, they had no idea what it was. In fact, the Hebrew word for manna means "What is it?"[1]

When the Israelites needed God to provide food in the wilderness, they didn't expect manna—but manna was exactly what they needed. Manna had 100 percent of the recommended daily nutrients for wandering in the wilderness. Has God ever provided something for you that was not what you expected? I know He has for me. But even though it wasn't what I expected, it was exactly what I needed.

Philippians 4:19 says, "And my God shall supply all your need according to His riches in glory by Christ Jesus." The manna in the golden jar is a reminder that we can trust Jehovah Jireh, the Lord who provides, to keep His promise to provide for us. That makes me want to stop and give God praise for His goodness.

POWER, LIFE, AND FREEDOM

The final thing in the ark of the covenant underneath the mercy seat was Aaron's rod that budded. This is amazing to me. Do you remember the story of when Moses and Aaron went before Pharaoh? God knew Pharaoh was going to ask for a miracle to back up their claims that the Lord had sent them.

> Then the LORD spoke to Moses and Aaron, saying, "When Pharaoh speaks to you, saying, 'Show a miracle for yourselves,' then you shall say to Aaron, 'Take your rod and cast it before Pharaoh, and let it become a serpent.'" So Moses and Aaron went in to Pharaoh, and they did so, just as the LORD commanded. And Aaron cast down his rod before Pharaoh and before his servants, and it became a serpent.

Pharaoh called in his sorcerers and magicians, and their rods became snakes when they threw them down too. But do you remember what happened next? The snake that was Aaron's rod swallowed up all the other snakes. The power of God triumphed over the power of the devil.

The fact that Aaron's rod is in the ark with the stone tablets and the jar of manna points us to this reality: The mercy seat gives us power over the devil. The mercy seat gives us power over the enemy. If it weren't for God's miracle mercy, the snakes would have killed you a long time ago. They would have sunk their fangs into you or choked the life out of you or swallowed you right up. Oh, but we have mercy.

Lamentations 3:22 says, "Through the LORD's mercies we are not consumed, because His compassions fail not." Because of His great mercy, the Lord isn't going to let the devil consume you. He isn't going to let the enemy choke the life out of you. He isn't going to let the enemy poison your joy. Many times you should have been defeated, but God's mercy gave you victory and swallowed every attack of the enemy.

Everything may not be perfect in your life, but if the devil had had his way, you would have been defeated and destroyed and consumed long ago. The devil came to steal, kill, and destroy. But God came to give you life—and not just any kind of life but abundant life. He came to give you hope. He came to give you joy. He came to give you purpose. And oh, precious, He came to show you mercy. And because of that mercy, you can walk in victory.

Because of God's mercy, you are more than a conqueror. It is all because of His mercy. It's not because of your goodness. It's not because of your money. It's not because of your skin color. It's not because of your education or your good looks or your big accomplishments in life. It's all because of His mercy. God's mercy swallowed up the attack of the enemy in your life.

Aaron's rod was used over and over again when the Lord was delivering the children of Israel from their bondage in Egypt. That is a good reminder too. Because of His mercy, God doesn't want His children living in bondage. His miracle mercy can set you free. So I ask you, What are you in bondage to? What is holding you captive? Whatever it is—drug addiction, pornography, envy, anxiety, depression, rejection, etc.— there is freedom waiting at the mercy seat. Whatever it is, God's mercy has it covered.

We know that everything in the tabernacle points to Jesus Christ. Galatians 5:1 says, "It was for freedom that Christ set us free" (NASB). Your freedom has already been bought and paid for. You have already been set free by the finished work of Jesus on the cross, so it's time to walk in that freedom. It's time to walk in victory.

After the children of Israel were delivered from bondage in Egypt, Aaron's rod made one more appearance before it was put into the ark underneath the mercy seat. While the children of Israel were still wandering in the wilderness, there was a rebellion. We talked about it earlier. Korah and some other leaders rebelled against Moses, and the ground swallowed them up. Then the people started complaining—again—and the Lord sent a plague that was only stopped by Aaron interceding for the people by bringing a censer of incense among them. In the aftermath, God decided to give the children of Israel a clear sign that He had chosen the tribe of Levi to be priests and to serve in the tabernacle.

The Lord told Moses to get one rod from the head of each tribe and write each man's name on his rod. Aaron's rod was used to represent the tribe of Levi. The rods were placed in the tabernacle, in the holy of holies. The Lord said, "And it shall be that the rod of the man whom I choose will blossom; thus I will rid Myself of the complaints of the children of Israel, which they make against you" (Num. 17:5). When Moses went into the tabernacle the next day, "the rod of Aaron, of the house of Levi, had sprouted and put forth buds, had produced blossoms and yielded ripe almonds" (v. 8). Aaron's rod budded, clearly marking him as God's choice as priest.

And do you know what? You have been chosen too. You have been chosen by a holy God to serve Him. You have been chosen to be part of His royal priesthood. And you have been chosen to receive mercy.

> But you are a chosen generation, a royal priesthood, a holy nation, His own special people, that you may proclaim the praises of Him who called you out of darkness into His marvelous light; who once were not a people but are now the people of God, who had not obtained mercy but now have obtained mercy.
>
> —1 PETER 2:9–10

Now, Aaron's rod budded, but it didn't stop with buds. There was a progression: buds, blossoms, and almonds. So there was a bud, then the flower, then the fruit. The bud represents God the Father. He's the foundation of it all. Nothing happens without the goodness of God the Father. He's the source of power. He's the source of it all. Some people ask me, "Jim Raley, how in the world have you made it? How did you come through what you've come through? How have you seen what you've seen and done what you've done?" I'll tell you right now: It's because I've had a greater source than myself. I depended on the Father.

Then there's the flower on Aaron's rod. The flower represents the Son, Jesus. The flower is fragrant. The flower is beautiful. How many of you can say your life smells a whole lot better because of Jesus? How many of you can say Jesus Christ has made something beautiful out of your life? How many of you can say that He has given you beauty for ashes? I'm telling you, I'm thankful for Jesus.

Then there's the fruit, the almond, on Aaron's rod. The fruit represents the Holy Spirit. I declare over you by faith that you're entering into a season of fruitfulness. You may be looking around your life right now and thinking, "There sure is a lot of dead stuff around here." You might want to tell me, "Well, Apostle Raley, you just don't understand. It's dead." That marriage is dead. That opportunity is dead. That door is dead. That issue is dead.

You need to understand something very important about Aaron's rod. It was dead. It had been cut from a tree. It was not connected to a tree anymore. It was a dead branch. It had no roots. It wasn't planted in the ground. It was disconnected. It was a dead piece of wood. But even though it was dead, it budded and bore fruit. Even though it was dead, it produced life. That tells us it doesn't matter how dead or disconnected something looks—mercy can bring it back to life.

That's the kind of thing that happens in the realm of no explanation. Mercy can bring that marriage back to life. Mercy can bring that relationship with your child back to life. Mercy can bring that ministry back to life. Mercy can bring your hope back to life. Mercy can bring your opportunities back to life. Mercy can bring your purpose back to life.

I know hell is mad right now because when I say stuff like this, the devil wishes I would shut up. But I am here to tell you that my God specializes in turning crucifixions into resurrections. Hallelujah! No matter what is dead in your life, God can bring it back to life.

Now watch this: I was studying about almond trees, and I learned it can take as long as three to twelve years for an almond tree to bear fruit. That is a long time. You can plant an almond tree and have a baby at the same time, and your baby could be in preschool, elementary school, or maybe even middle school by the time the tree starts to produce fruit. But the Bible says that when they put the rods in front of the mercy seat, Aaron's rod budded overnight.

You see, God's mercy brings fruitfulness and resurrection quickly. I declare in the mighty name of Jesus that God is about to expedite things in your life. You've been waiting long enough. God is about to speed things up. What you thought was going to take years will happen overnight. God will do it overnight. He will change your children overnight. He will change your family overnight. He will bring that person back overnight. He will restore what you thought was hopelessly dead overnight. God doesn't need years to bring something dead back to life. He can do it in an instant. Praise the Lord!

WHERE'S YOUR FOCUS?

The Israelites didn't stay in one spot. They were wandering in the wilderness, not just camping. And whenever they broke camp and moved to a new location, the ark of the covenant went first. It was always in front as they journeyed to a new place. When the ark moved out, they moved out behind it. When the ark stopped, they stopped.

When it was time to enter the Promised Land, the ark of the covenant went first. The children of Israel had to cross the Jordan River to get into the Promised Land, and as soon as the priests bearing the ark set foot in the Jordan, the water stopped coming from upstream, and the people were able to cross over on dry ground.

When the children of Israel went into battle against the walled city of Jericho, the Lord told them to march around the city with the ark leading the way. And we all know what the end result of that battle was: The walls came tumbling down.

Here's the point: When the people of Israel were on a journey, or they needed a miracle, or they were facing a seemingly impossible battle, the ark was in front. It was in their line of vision. It was where their focus was.

For the Israelites, keeping their focus on the ark of the covenant and the mercy seat was a constant reminder of the goodness of God. It was a reminder of His faithfulness. It was a reminder of His Word, written on two stone tablets. It was a reminder that His mercy covered their sin. It was a reminder of His miraculous provision, even when they didn't deserve it. It was a reminder of all He had done to see them free from bondage. It was a reminder that the power of God triumphs over the power of the enemy. It was a reminder that He brings dead things back to life. It was a reminder of all the things that mercy had done in their lives. It was a reminder that God does miracles. It was a reminder that God is not bound by the natural order of the world; He is supernatural, so He can do the unexplainable.

So often we lose focus. We take our eyes off Jesus. We take our eyes off the truth. We let the schemes and wiles of that crafty old devil get us distracted. But just as the children of Israel needed to keep their eyes on the ark and the mercy seat and all they represented as they journeyed or battled, we need to keep our eyes on Jesus. The ark and the mercy seat point straight to Jesus. They point straight to His work on the cross at Calvary. They point straight to the truth of everything He did for us, provided for us, and blessed us with, all because He loves us and wants to connect with us. The Book of Hebrews reminds us to look to Jesus, "the author and finisher of our faith" (12:2). So I ask you this, precious: Where's your focus?

Just as the children of Israel needed to keep their eyes on the ark and the mercy seat and all they represented, we need to keep our eyes on Jesus.

The mercy seat is a reminder of the truth. The Lord is abundant in mercy. His grace is sufficient for us. He removes our sins from us as far as the east is from the west. We are chosen. We are accepted. We can walk in freedom. We can walk in victory. No weapon formed against us will prosper. We are more than conquerors. We can go boldly before the throne of grace to find help whenever we need it. We are loved. Praise the Lord!

PRAYER

Lord Jesus, I am thankful for Your glory that will light up even the darkest places in my life. You are the Savior, the Healer, the Redeemer, the Ancient of Days. You are the God who sees and the Lord who sanctifies. You are the Messiah. You are Immanuel. I will praise Your holy name forever, Jesus.

God, I am so thankful for Your mercy that covers all my sin. You knew I would miss the mark and cross the line, but You provided a way for me to still come into Your presence. You provided a way for me to connect with You. You provided all the grace, mercy, and forgiveness I could ever need. Thank You, Lord! I also thank You for Your provision. Even when I didn't deserve it, even when I messed up, You were still so good to me. You are a good Father, and I praise You for supplying all my need.

I thank You for setting me free, Lord. I thank You for the power to overcome the enemy. I thank You for the victory You won on the cross. Because of Your mercy, I am more than a conqueror. Because of Your mercy, I walk in freedom. Thank You for being my source. Thank You for giving me abundant life. Thank You for bringing the dead things in my life back to life.

Lord, I declare today that I will keep my focus on You. I will fix my eyes on You. I will remember the truth. I will remember Your mercy, Your goodness,

Your provision, and Your power. I will remember how much You love me, and I will walk in victory in the name of Jesus! Hallelujah!

Chapter 11

MIRACLE MERCY

Let Your mercy, O LORD, be upon us, just as we hope in You.
—PSALM 33:22

EHIND THE VEIL, inside the holy of holies, inside the place where the presence and glory of the Lord God Almighty manifested on the earth, on top of the ark of the covenant, was the mercy seat. The Hebrew word for mercy seat is *kapōret*.[1] It comes from the root word *kāpar*, which means to cover. The mercy seat was literally a cover for the ark; it was a lid. But the mercy seat covered so much more than the ark, for *kāpar* also means to make atonement, to cleanse, to expiate, to cancel, to pardon, to forgive, to put off, to pacify, and to reconcile.[2]

The mercy seat was the symbol of God's willingness to forgive—His willingness to pardon us for all we have done that goes against His Word, His willingness to cancel our debt of sin, His willingness to reconcile us with Himself. It represents His willingness to cover all our mistakes, mishaps, and mess-ups with His abundant mercy. God knew that our sins and transgressions would separate us from Him, so the mercy seat is a powerful symbol of this truth: God wants to connect with us. He wants us to enter the realm of no explanation.

WORSHIP IN THE PRESENCE

On the Day of Atonement, the one day a year that the high priest performed his duties inside the holy of holies, he first entered with a bucket of fire.

> Then he shall take a censer full of burning coals of fire from the altar before the LORD, with his hands full of sweet incense beaten fine, and bring it inside the veil. And he shall put the incense on the fire before the LORD, that the cloud of incense may cover the mercy seat that is on the Testimony, lest he die.
>
> —LEVITICUS 16:12–13

The mercy seat was the symbol of God's willingness to cover all our mistakes, mishaps, and mess-ups with His abundant mercy.

The presence of the Lord was so intense, so powerful, that it needed to be dimmed by the smoke of the incense. When Moses asked the Lord to show him His glory, the Lord said, "You cannot see My face; for no man shall see Me, and live" (Exod. 33:20). The Lord hid Moses in the cleft of a rock and covered him with His hand as He passed by, but He provided another way for someone to be in His presence in the holy of holies.

Remember, the incense represents

worship. It represents prayer. When the high priest entered the holy of holies with the bucket of fire and put the incense on the fire, it was like the worship and prayers of the people rising up before the Lord.

When the priest entered the holy of holies, he would encounter the two angels, or cherubim, on the mercy seat.

> You shall make a mercy seat of pure gold; two and a half cubits shall be its length and a cubit and a half its width. And you shall make two cherubim of gold; of hammered work you shall make them at the two ends of the mercy seat. Make one cherub at one end, and the other cherub at the other end; you shall make the cherubim at the two ends of it of one piece with the mercy seat. And the cherubim shall stretch out their wings above, covering the mercy seat with their wings, and they shall face one another; the faces of the cherubim shall be toward the mercy seat. You shall put the mercy seat on top of the ark, and in the ark you shall put the Testimony that I will give you. And there I will meet with you, and I will speak with you from above the mercy seat, from between the two cherubim which are on the ark of the Testimony, about everything which I will give you in commandment to the children of Israel.
>
> —Exodus 25:17–22

This is where it gets real. The angels also represent worship. Angels worship the Lord. The throne room in heaven is full of angels who fall on their faces before the Lord, saying things like, "Blessing and glory and wisdom, thanksgiving and honor and power and might, be to our God forever and ever. Amen," and "Holy, holy, holy is the LORD of hosts; the whole earth is full of His glory!" (Rev. 7:12; Isa. 6:3). The angels on the mercy seat point us to worship.

The Bible says the angels on the mercy seat were of hammered or beaten work. They were not cast. They were not preformed. They were beaten. They endured hammer blows. They endured the fire. And it was the hammer blows and the fire that positioned them as worshippers in the presence of the Lord.

Here's the point: The devil is dumb. He's not just some dumb; he's plumb dumb. The devil thinks that when he inflicts hammer blows on our lives and puts us through the fire we will turn away from God. He thinks every time we go through a hard season or a hard time, we're going to turn away from God. But we know the truth. The Lord said, "Fear not, for I have redeemed you; I have called you by your name; you are Mine. When you pass through the waters, I will be with you; and through the rivers, they shall not overflow you. When you walk through the fire, you shall not be burned, nor shall the flame scorch you. For I am the LORD your God, the Holy One of Israel, your Savior" (Isa. 43:1–3).

The devil may put us through the fire and try to beat us down with his hammer blows, but every time he hits us, every blow points us to the mercy seat. Every blow, every moment in the fire, is preparing us to worship. We bring our tattered wings, and we worship together. Life hasn't been perfect for any of us; we all face seasons of fire and beatings. But the hard times turn us all the more to the mercy seat, to the presence of the Lord. We know that because of Jesus we have access to the throne and we can boldly approach it to "obtain mercy and find grace to help in time of need" (Heb. 4:16). And what can our response be but worship?

Yes, we'll have hard times. Sometimes worship is beaten

work. Sometimes it's hard. But we say, "Lord, I'm not going to let it make me bitter. I'm not going to let it separate me from You." There have been times in my life when the devil thought he was winning, but God was only using my struggle to get me focused on Him. That's when I say, "Oh, devil, you tried your best. You brought everything you could against me, but how do you like me now? Hallelujah! I've turned toward the mercy seat."

JUSTICE AND RIGHTEOUSNESS, JUDGMENT AND MERCY

After creating the cloud of smoke with the censer of fire and incense, the high priest entered the holy of holies with a bucket of blood. In the description of the equipment needed for the brazen altar in Exodus 27:3, the term used is "basins," or *mizrāq* in the Hebrew.[3] The root word of mizrāq is *zāraq*, which means to scatter or sprinkle,[4] so the basins were used for the purpose of sprinkling the blood of the sacrifices rather than for other purposes, like cleaning up.

The priest actually had to enter the holy of holies more than once with a bucket of blood. Before entering the holy of holies to create the cloud of smoke with the incense, he would slaughter a bull. After he created the cloud, he would reenter the holy of holies with a bucket of blood from the bull to atone for himself and his house (his family). Then he would go back out, and lots would be cast to determine which of two goats would be sacrificed to atone for the sins of the people. One goat was sacrificed and its blood was applied to the mercy seat inside the holy of holies, while the other goat, the scapegoat, was released into the wilderness.

There was a very specific process for the Day of Atonement laid out in Leviticus 16. So the high priest carried a basin or bucket of blood into the holy of holies twice on the Day of Atonement.

The bucket used to carry the blood into the holy of holies was pointed on the bottom. The priest could never set that bucket of blood down inside the veil. He could use it to sprinkle the mercy seat with blood, but he could never set it down—because the work was never done. A year later, on the Day of Atonement, the high priest would have to go into the holy of holies again, and then again a year after that.

This would have had to continue on and on and on forever, but God had a different plan in mind. He wanted to be able to connect with each of us personally. He wanted everyone to be able to enter His presence, not just the high priest. He wanted us to be able to fellowship with Him all the time, not just once a year. That is why He sent Jesus.

The high priest couldn't sit down inside the holy of holies. He couldn't sit in the mercy seat because he wasn't worthy. He couldn't sit down in the presence of the Lord. He had sinned, and when he entered the holy of holies with a basin of blood for the first time, it was to make atonement for himself. He couldn't even make atonement for the children of Israel as a whole until he dealt with his own sin, his own issues, his own need for mercy. He sacrificed a bull to make atonement for himself and sprinkled its blood on and before the mercy seat.

But two thousand years ago, God's plan came about. Jesus, the Lamb of God who takes away the sins of the world, the "great High Priest," the "High Priest who...was in all points tempted as we are, yet without sin," gave His blood on the cross at Calvary (Heb. 4:14–15). And do you know where He is right now? He's seated at the right hand of the Father. The great High Priest is sitting down in the presence of the Lord because the work is done. Atonement no longer has to be made over and over and over again. Once Jesus did it, it never had to be done again! As Jesus Himself said, "It is finished!" (John 19:30).

We already talked about how the two angels, the cherubim, on the mercy seat represent worship. But that isn't the only thing they represent. One angel represents the justice of God, and one angel represents the righteousness of God. Remember, the ark of the covenant represents God's throne on earth, and the Word says, "Righteousness and justice are the foundation of [God's] throne" (Ps. 89:14). "He loves righteousness and justice" (Ps. 33:5), and they are both essential parts of His holiness.

So here you are, right smack in the middle of God's justice and God's righteousness. Because God is holy, only the righteous can stand before Him. Because He is holy, justice must be served. So how do you stand? When you look at God's righteousness, you know you don't come anywhere close to measuring up. You fully understand the truth of the verse saying that "all our righteousnesses are like filthy rags" (Isa. 64:6). You know you've been unrighteous. You know you have failed. You know you've missed the mark and crossed the line. But you also know that righteousness demands justice. Your failure demands a sacrifice.

So you have righteousness on one side and justice on the other. What do you do when you are faced with God's righteousness and justice? How do you make it? How do you survive? I'll tell you: There is only one way. You have to get mercy in the middle. Do you know what's between the righteousness of God and the justice of God? It's mercy. Mercy is in the middle. I wouldn't be here today if mercy hadn't gotten in the middle. You and I both deserve judgment, but mercy got in the middle. Hallelujah!

We've been talking about the mercy seat, but you need to know there is also a judgment seat. Second Corinthians 5:10 says, "For we must all appear before the judgment seat of Christ." We know that "God is a just judge" and "He shall judge the world in righteousness" (Ps. 7:11; 9:8).

Because God is a just Judge who judges in righteousness, He would have to judge us all guilty if we stood before Him on our own merits. If I had to depend on my own righteousness, my own holiness, my own works, I would be in deep, deep trouble. I don't even want to think about how long my sentence would be. I don't even want to think about what it would be like to be separated from the Lord forever because of my sin. But God didn't want you to be separated from Him forever. That's why He made a way for the judgment seat to be turned into the mercy seat.

When the priest entered the holy of holies, he was facing the judgment seat. But the moment the blood hit it, the moment he sprinkled the blood of the sacrifice, the judgment seat changed to a mercy seat. It works the same with us. We deserve judgment, but because of the power of the blood, we get mercy instead. We deserve judgment for all our trespasses and transgressions, but the precious blood of Jesus Christ covered them all. Because of the blood, the just and righteous Judge of all the earth can look at us and pronounce, "Not guilty!"

Let me ask you something: What are you building in your life—a judgment seat or a mercy seat? What are you building with your Facebook account? What are you building with your social media? What are you building with your attitudes, your actions, and your words? Are you building a judgment seat or a mercy seat?

The Word of God warns us over and over again about judging others, because there is only one Judge. Jesus said, "Judge not, that you be not judged. For with what judgment you judge, you will be judged; and with the measure you use, it will be measured back to you" (Matt. 7:1–2). Paul wrote to the church in Rome, "Therefore let us not judge one another anymore, but rather resolve this, not to put a stumbling block or a cause to fall in our brother's way" (Rom. 14:13).

We need to leave the judgment up to God. He is the righteous Judge. Instead of building a judgment seat in my life, I'm going to build a mercy seat. I know my sins have been covered by the blood, so I'm not going to spend my time judging people. I need mercy too much in my life.

> **The devil is the prince of the power of the air. Never forget for a moment that a prince is always subject to a king.**

The ark of the covenant had a molding of gold all the way around, like a crown, just like some of the other furniture in the tabernacle. And a crown points to a king. In the tabernacle, there is only one king that everything points to. His name is King Jesus. He is the King of kings and Lord of lords. He is the ruler over all the earth. And do you know who that sneaky old devil is, the one who is always trying to mess with you? The devil is the prince of the power of the air. Never forget for a moment that a prince is always subject to a king.

When that devil is trying to mess you up and stress you out and press you down, you just remind him that you belong to the King! King Jesus has already won the victory over hell, death, and the grave; the devil just doesn't want to admit it yet. When the devil comes to remind you of all the times you have failed, all the times you have sinned, all the times you have done something you shouldn't have, you just tell him, "The blood of King Jesus has got me covered!"

Do you remember the story of Cain and Abel? After Cain killed his brother, the Lord told Cain, "The voice of your brother's blood cries out to Me from the ground" (Gen. 4:10). The blood was crying out to the Lord; it was crying out for judgment, for vengeance, for revenge.

Cain was judged, and he lived his entire life as a fugitive and vagabond on the earth. But that was before Jesus and even before the tabernacle. Remember, "without shedding of blood there is no remission" (Heb. 9:22). But God took care of that, once and for all, when Jesus shed His blood on the cross at Calvary. The Word says this:

> But you have come to Mount Zion and to the city of the living God, the heavenly Jerusalem, to an innumerable company of angels, to the general assembly and church of the firstborn who are registered in heaven, to God the Judge of all, to the spirits of just men made perfect, to Jesus the Mediator of the new covenant, and to the blood of sprinkling that speaks better things than that of Abel.
> —HEBREWS 12:22–24

Is God still the Judge? Yes, of course He is. He is "the Judge of all." He is holy and righteous, so it has to be that way. But Jesus is the Mediator. He is the One who acts as a go-between, who intervenes in situations to restore relationships, to make peace, to reconcile people. And when Jesus' blood was shed, it cried out to the Lord too. But because Jesus was the perfect, sinless sacrifice, it cried out for "better things" than Abel's blood did.

Instead of crying out for revenge, the blood of Jesus cried out for forgiveness. Instead of crying out for vengeance, it cried out for grace. Instead of crying out for judgment, it cried out for mercy. The blood of Jesus cries out from the ground at Calvary and says, "Forgive them. Restore them. Reconcile them. Put them back together again. Deliver them from drugs. Deliver them from sexual sin. Deliver them from bondage to iniquity. Set them free. Give them peace. Forgive them for all that they did." Praise the Lord!

> *Instead of crying out for revenge, the blood of Jesus cried out for forgiveness. Instead of crying out for vengeance, it cried out for grace.*

LOVE IS RED

Do you need a breakthrough? Meet me at the mercy seat. Do you need healing? Meet me at the mercy seat. Do your children need to be saved? Meet me at the mercy seat. Do you need to be set free from addiction? Meet me at the mercy seat. Do you need relationships restored or reconciled? Meet me at the mercy seat.

The mercy seat is the place of miracles. It is the realm of no explanation. Mercy in and of itself is a miracle because we definitely don't deserve it. If you need a miracle, the mercy seat is where you will find it.

Do you know what the real power behind the mercy seat is? Do you know what's behind all the miracles? It's love—and that is why I'm telling you that love is red. Love is what opens up the mercy seat.

What is the reason that God decided to show us mercy? Love.

The reason Jesus died on the cross at Calvary? Love.

The reason the Lord wants us to walk in freedom and victory? Love.

The reason God wants our relationships with other people restored? Love.

The reason God wants your children saved? Love.

The reason God wants you to connect with Him? Love.

The reason God works miracles in your life? Love.

It's all about love, for "God is love" (1 John 4:8). And love is red.

You may be thinking, "What does all that have to do with the color of love being red?" Let me tell you. I know that all different kinds of people can love. I know black people can love, white people can love, and brown people can love. But that's not the ultimate love because you could love somebody this week and not be able to stand that person next week. You might love somebody with all your heart, but then you read something they wrote on Facebook, and all of a sudden you don't love them so much anymore. As humans, our love is often conditional. But God's love isn't like that. It is the red blood of Jesus that's the greatest love of all.

Understand me, please. Hear my heart. When you get underneath the skin, underneath the epidermis, we all are pretty much alike. It doesn't matter what color you are on the outside. We all have hearts that beat. We all have minds that think. We all have veins that carry blood. Underneath the skin, we are the same. It doesn't matter who you are. It doesn't matter what color you are. It doesn't matter what class you are. It doesn't matter what your financial condition is. It doesn't matter what your educational background is. It doesn't even matter how spiritual you are. The truth is, we all need miracle mercy. And miracle mercy was bought with the precious blood of Jesus Christ, and blood is red. That is why I say that love is red.

Let me tell you, in this crazy world we live in, with all the strife and hatred and bitterness being stirred up right and left over things that shouldn't matter, when the body of Christ comes together as one—men, women, and children of all races, cultures, backgrounds, socioeconomic statuses, etc.— to walk in unity, reconciliation, forgiveness, understanding, and peace, it is a miracle straight from the heart of God and straight from the realm of no explanation.

The world will try to tell you there is too much hurt, too much hatred, too much hardness of heart for a diverse group of people to walk in unity. They will try to tell you it's impossible. But with God all things are possible. There is nothing too hard for Him.

The world may look at the body of Christ walking in unity and say we must be drinking too much of the Kool-Aid or something like that because they can't explain it. But there is an explanation: It comes from the realm of no explanation. It is supernatural. It is the power of the mercy of a gracious God healing wounds; restoring relationships; rooting out bitterness; and filling hearts with love, peace, and hope. Mercy has got it covered.

So here's what I have to tell you: Just meet me at the mercy seat. Don't act like you've got it going on; just meet me at the mercy seat. Don't act like you're better than anybody else; just meet me at the mercy seat. Don't act like you've never struggled; just meet me at the mercy seat. It doesn't matter what you've done. It doesn't matter how you've struggled. Ultimate love can be found today at the mercy seat, and that is the greatest miracle of all.

PRAYER

*Lord, I declare now that when the devil tries to
beat me up and beat me down and put me through
the fire, I will just praise You all the more. I know
You will always be with me, even in the fire, so I
praise Your name! Great is the Lord and worthy to
be praised! Blessing and glory and wisdom, thanksgiving and honor and power and might, be to You,
God, forever and ever! Holy are You, Lord of hosts;
the whole earth is full of Your glory!*

*Lord, I thank You that miracles are going to man-
ifest in my life that I don't deserve, but the miracles are coming because of Your great mercy and
because the blood has covered the mercy seat. I
know, Lord, that when You bless me, You don't bless
me because I'm worthy. You bless me because when
You look at me, all You see is the blood of Jesus, and
You bless me because You love me. Thank You, Lord,
that I am washed in the blood of the Lamb.*

*Lord, I ask You to pour out Your love and mercy
on Your people. Let Your miracle mercy at work in
our lives show the world that You love them, that
You are love. Let me build a mercy seat in my life
rather than a judgment seat. I need Your mercy,
and others needs it too, so let me never be a stumbling block by being judgmental. Let me remember
every moment of every day that love is red.*

*I cover my family in the blood of Jesus. I cover my
children and grandchildren in the blood. I cover my
marriage in the blood. I cover my job in the blood. I*

cover my church in the blood. I cover my ministry in the blood. Then, Lord, I call down the fire. I call the fire of the Holy Ghost. I call for an outpouring of the Spirit in my home, in my community, in my church, in my city. I praise You in advance for all that Your miracle-working power is going to do! Thank You, Lord Jesus!

JimRaleyBooks.com/chp11

Chapter 12

UNCOMMON ANOINTING

I have been anointed with fresh oil.
—Psalm 92:10

THE JOURNEY THROUGH the tabernacle is all about getting to the holy of holies, the realm of no explanation. It's about the Creator of the entire universe wanting to connect with each of us on a personal level. The Lord loves you, and He wants to be in relationship with you so you will recognize His hand behind the unexplainable things in your life.

The truth is that we need the power of God at work in our lives. We need miracles from the realm of no explanation. We need the mercy seat. We need the glory of the Lord moving in our midst. Wherever you are in life, whatever circumstances you are facing, however the enemy is coming against you to try to bring you down, you need the wonderworking power of Jesus Christ at work in your life.

The Process

Remember, the key to getting to the holy of holies is the process. Start by building your life around the presence of the Lord. This is no time to put God in second place. There is a fierce battle being waged against you, against your children, against your family, against the body of Christ. It's time to stop messing around. You need Jesus right smack-dab in the center of your life.

Put all the things in your life that need to die on the altar, and let them die. And then watch as the Lord brings back to life the things you need but thought were gone forever.

Then it's time to approach the gate with praise. Be thankful to the Lord and bless His name. If you love Him, give Him praise right now. Thank the Healer, the Deliverer, the Provider, the Baptizer, the Sanctifier, the Ancient of Days. He is the Holy One, the Mighty One of Israel, Wonderful, Counselor, Mighty God, Everlasting Father, Prince of Peace, Captain of the Host, Lily of the Valley, Bright and Morning Star, Fairest of Ten Thousand; the Way, the Truth, and the Life. He is Isaac's ram, Job's Redeemer, Abraham's seed, the seed of the woman, the conquering King, the coming King, the risen Savior, the Lord of all, the unstoppable Jesus. There is no one like Him. Lift your voice! Clap your hands! Shout unto God with a voice of triumph! He is worthy of all our praise!

Then it's time to approach the altar. Lay down all the junk in your trunk and let God put your sin into remission. It's time to know and accept that you have been justified by the sacrifice of the Lamb of God. You have been washed in the blood, and your sins have been removed as far as the east is from the west. Put all the things in your life that need to die on the altar, and let them die. And then watch as the Lord brings back to life the things you need but thought were gone forever. Hallelujah! After that, it's time to offer yourself as a living sacrifice, holy and acceptable to God—because the offering, the sacrifice, that God wants more than anything is *you*.

Next you need to approach the brazen laver. It is time to be sanctified, set apart by the washing of the water of the Word. It's time to come clean, precious. Stop pretending the dirt you see on your face when you look into the mirror of the Word isn't there. It's time to let the Word be big in your life! If you want to operate in the realm of no explanation, the Word needs to be big in your life. You need to read it, meditate on it, get it in your head, write it on your heart, and let it come out of your mouth. There are no words more powerful than the ones in the Word. If you want mercy seat miracles, you need the Word.

Then it is time to walk past the five pillars marking the entrance to the holy place, remembering the Lord is Wonderful, Counselor, Mighty God, Everlasting Father, and Prince of Peace. You have to know that you know that you know who God is and all that He can do. You have to know that God is true to His Word. You have to know that God is who He says He is—Wonderful, Counselor, Mighty God, Everlasting Father, Prince of Peace—because that's what is holding you up.

Then it's time to enter the holy place. You see the golden lampstand, reminding you that you need a source. You need the oil of the Holy Spirit. You need a continual replenishing of the oil of the Holy Ghost. And you need the light so you can see the bread. You need the light in order to see the table inviting you to be refreshed and renewed by spending time in the presence of the Lord and in His Word. Remember that the bread is always available. Remember that your purpose is to be a dancing vessel, allowing the Lord to lead.

The last stop before you enter the holy of holies is the altar of incense. It is a place of worship. It is a place of intercession. It is the place you offer up your anyhow worship—no matter your circumstances, you are going to worship the Lord anyhow. No matter how beaten you are, you are going to be a worshipper.

Then you pass through the veil, the one that was torn from top to bottom the moment Jesus died and forever gave free and open access to whoever would believe in Him. And then you are there, inside the holy of holies, the realm of no explanation, the place of mercy seat miracles.

THE ANOINTING

During the time of the wilderness tabernacle, only one person had access to the holy of holies: the high priest. When the tabernacle was first built, the high priest was Aaron. He and his sons were chosen to be priests for the Israelites, but only Aaron could go before the mercy seat. Only Aaron could encounter the manifest presence of God behind the veil. Only Aaron could be in the realm of the miraculous and unexplainable.

Understand that all the priests were anointed. The Lord told Moses, "Clothe your brother, Aaron, and his sons with these garments, and then anoint and ordain them. Consecrate them so they can serve as my priests" (Exod. 28:41, NLT). When the scripture says, "...anoint and ordain them," it is referring to an anointing that was made available to every priest. This was a common anointing that all priests received. This anointing was a prerequisite for these men to fulfill the duties of a priest. This anointing provided them access to the outer court and the inner court, but the holy of holies was off-limits for these guys.

The holy of holies, or the realm of no explanation, could only be accessed by one man, Aaron. It's important to note that Aaron received a separate anointing from the rest of the priesthood: "You shall put the holy garments on Aaron, and anoint him and consecrate him, that he may minister to Me as priest" (Exod. 40:13).

In Exodus 28:41 the pronoun *them* was used, but in Exodus 40:13 the personal pronoun *him* is used. This anointing was a separate anointing from the regular priesthood. This uncommon anointing granted access to the holy of holies, where the miraculous occurred. It was the place of no explanation and could only be accessed by the one who had been anointed with an uncommon anointing.

Most believers live their lives with just a common anointing, satisfied to live where everything is obtainable and explainable by natural phenomena. When we do this, most of our lives are lived in the outer court. Just as the priest ministered in natural light, so are our lives lived in the natural. We are saved, but if we can't see, touch, feel, hear, or taste it, we don't experience it.

Then there are believers who seem to mature and move into a deeper experience with God. When they do this, they move to the inner court, or the holy place. In the inner court are the table of showbread, the golden lampstand, and the altar of incense, pointing to the light and oil of the Holy Spirit, the Word of God, and worship.

It is a blessing to move into a closer relationship with God, to become hungry for the bread of His Word, eager for His light of guidance and the oil of His Spirit, and more fervent in worship. It is a wonderful and precious thing. But inner court believers still have one foot in the outer court and still depend on man because they need a man to bring them oil and bread. Just as the priest depended on a man to bring him the bread and the oil, many believers still have a dependency on the things of this world to sustain them. But I don't want to be an inner court believer. I want more.

I don't want to stay in the outer court. I don't want to stay in the inner court. I want to go deeper. I want to go further. I want to see the glory of God for myself. I want to encounter the presence of the Lord. I want to experience the power of my wonder-working God in the realm of no explanation. I want an uncommon anointing.

There are a precious few who get in a position to receive an uncommon anointing, and for them everything changes. This uncommon anointing ushers them into the atmosphere of the holy of holies. In this realm man provides nothing. God provides it all! It's a place where we do not rely, count, or depend on the hand of man but the hand of God.

God desires to anoint common men and women with an uncommon anointing. When something is uncommon, it is often more precious and valuable. To see the uncommon is to experience the rare, to witness something not frequently seen or expected. It is not routine or mundane, but it is unusual and remarkable. So it is with the uncommon anointing. It is extremely rare, and that rareness makes it ever so valuable. In the life of a believer, receiving the uncommon anointing is the first and critical step into the uncommon life.

The anointings in the Bible were very sacred and important. When someone was fortunate enough to be anointed, it was a beautiful, wonderful, and mysterious thing. The anointing was prized and precious because it carried with it great significance, as it related to the assignment and destiny of the one who was anointed.

There are fourteen different words used in the original texts of the Bible for the word *anoint* in all its forms (verb, noun, and adjective). In order to truly grasp the preciousness and power found in the anointing, we should look at the meanings of some of the words.

The first time we see a form of the word *anoint* in the Bible (in Genesis 31:13: "I am the God of Bethel, where you anointed the pillar and where you made a vow to Me"), it is the Hebrew word *māšah*. The word literally means to paint or smear, to spread over, "to draw the hand over," or "to rub with oil." It was considered both a covering and a consecration.[1] It is the word used for anoint in both Exodus 28:41 (anointing all the priests) and Exodus 40:13 (anointing the high priest, Aaron).

When a person was anointed, they were actually painted, covered, and smeared with the anointing oil. This word was even used to describe what ancient Jewish warriors did to their leather shields. They would anoint, or paint, their shields with oil, making the leather more tenacious and less vulnerable to attack. There was protection in the anointing. Never forget that when we receive a heavenly anointing, great protection comes along with it.

There are many who have walked in God's precious anointing and have been painted by His presence, and as a result they have survived relentless and intense attacks from the enemy. It brings to light afresh the powerful scripture penned by Isaiah that declares, "No weapon formed against you shall prosper" (Isa. 54:17). There are many assaults and attacks launched against God's anointed, but they have not and shall not prosper because there is protection in the anointing!

There have probably been times when you've faced powerful struggles in your own life, and as you look back, you wonder how you made it through. In the natural there seems to be no explanation—you made it through because you had the anointing of God. His precious anointing protected you, even when you didn't realize it.

Another powerful word that can be translated "anoint" is the Hebrew word *bālal*. For example, Psalm 92:10 uses the word *bālal*: "I have been anointed with fresh oil." It means to mix, mingle, blend, or combine.[2] I think that is incredible! When someone was anointed, it was considered a divine act. It meant that God's power and presence were combining and joining forces with the person being anointed!

When we receive a heavenly anointing, it is a supernatural occurrence. God unites our natural with His supernatural. He mixes, mingles, combines, and connects His power to our lives through the anointing. When this occurs, supernatural things begin to happen. Never lose sight of the fact that miracles live in the anointing!

The word *bālal* also means to confuse and confound.[3] Through the anointing, through the mixing and mingling of God's power in our lives, something very powerful happens. We are able to confuse and confound our enemy, the devil. All of a sudden we look different to him in the spirit realm. This must be incredibly disheartening and terrifying to the devil. He realizes it's us, but it isn't us—we are so much more when we are anointed!

It is wonderful to become so immersed in the anointing that Satan is threatened and confused by the magnitude of God's power resting on our lives. How desperately we need the bālal of God to come on our generation that we might confuse, confound, disrupt, and destroy every scheme of the enemy.

There is another glorious layer of revelation that must be brought to light as it relates to the word *bālal.* It also means "to fade away."[4] When we are anointed by God, it is for His glory and not ours. Our agenda and our plans all fade away. We are not anointed so we can be exalted but rather so the Lord can be exalted. It's impossible for egotistical people to maintain God's anointing for very long. Ego cries, "Look at me!" while anointing cries, "Look at Him!" True anointing gets every eye on Jesus. It is not about us; it's all about Him.

That's the kind of anointing I want. I want an uncommon anointing. I want an anointing that consecrates me for the Lord and protects me. I want an anointing that confuses the enemy. I want an anointing that keeps my focus off me and all on Jesus. I want an anointing that combines God's super with my natural so I can walk in the supernatural. I want an anointing that keeps me right in the middle of the realm of no explanation.

We are not anointed so we can be exalted but rather so the Lord can be exalted.

WHO'S GOT NEXT?

The reason I want the uncommon anointing is so much bigger than just my life. Do I need the mercy seat miracles in my life? Absolutely! But others need them too.

As believers walking in the uncommon anointing, we need to pass our faith on. We need to encourage other believers, especially the next generation, to build their lives around the presence of the Lord, to approach the gate with praise, lay it all on the altar, get washed by the water of the Word, be filled with the oil of the Holy Spirit to light the world on fire, to feast in and on God's presence, to worship the Lord for His greatness, and to pass through the veil into the holy of holies for themselves. We need to spur them on so they can experience the realm of no explanation for themselves, and in turn, they can pass on their faith.

It's like the Sea of Galilee/Dead Sea analogy. The two bodies of water are only about sixty-five miles apart. One, the Sea of Galilee, is fresh water, full of life. The other, the Dead Sea, is just that—dead. It is salt water with such a high concentration of salt that nothing can live in it. And do you know what makes the difference? They both have water coming in, but the Sea of Galilee has water flowing out of it and the Dead Sea doesn't.

When you have an uncommon anointing, you have all kinds of wonderful things flowing into your life. But if you don't have wonderful things flowing out of your life and into the lives of others, you will end up stagnant and dead. We need the good stuff coming in and flowing out of our lives.

As uncommon-anointing, realm-of-no-explanation believers, we need to be pouring into the next generation. Who's got next? You do! It's time to walk in the uncommon anointing not only for your own benefit but for the benefit of others God places in your path—and all for His glory.

So let me ask you, precious:

Have you built your life around God's presence?

Do you approach the Lord with praise and thankfulness?

Have you laid everything you need to get rid of on the altar?

Is your life a living sacrifice?

How big is the Word in your life?

Are you filled with the oil of the Holy Ghost?

Are you spending time face-to-face with the Lord and feasting on His Word?

Are you a worshipper?

If so, you are in the miracle zone, the realm of no explanation. There is no place like it. Get ready to see the supernatural operating in your life. I declare you are going to see mercy seat miracles.

Never disconnect from the journey. Keep entering into God's presence with thanksgiving. Keep yourself on the altar. Keep yourself in the Word. Stay amazed by the One called Wonderful, Counselor, Mighty God, Everlasting Father, Prince of Peace. Keep yourself in a position and in a place where you're full of oil and full of fire. Decide right now that the bread of His presence and the bread of His Word are going to be precious to you. Decide that the altar is for worshippers, and you're going to live as a worshipper. Cherish the gospel and live from the mercy seat, from the realm of no explanation.

PRAYER

Lord, I enter into Your presence, and I thank You. I praise Your glorious name. Lord, I want to build You a house with my praise because You inhabit the praises of Your people.

Lord, I come to the altar, and I thank You for the blood. I thank You for Jesus. I offer myself as a living sacrifice. I thank You that I'm cleansed and changed by Your Word. I thank You that You are Wonderful, Counselor, Mighty God, Everlasting Father, and Prince of Peace. I thank You that I'm full of oil and full of light and full of power. You're the Light of the world. I thank You that I have the bread of Your presence and the bread of Your Word. God, You guide me and direct me, and I bless Your name for it.

I thank You, God, that I am a worshipper and an intercessor. Hallelujah! I thank You for the gospel that changed my life. I thank You that the veil was torn so I can get to the mercy seat. I thank You that I have access to the realm of no explanation.

Move me out of my world and get me into Yours. Jesus, I need You. Move me out of my limitations. Move me out of my sickness and into Your healing. Move me out of my despair and into Your joy. Move me out of my bondage and into Your freedom. Move me out of my frustration and into Your breakthrough. Move me out of my world and put me into Yours.

Thank You, Jesus, for the tabernacle and the picture it paints of who You are. Consecrate me with Your uncommon anointing. Set me apart for You. I love You, Lord, and I want to be connected to You so that I can walk in the supernatural. Let me never forget that it's all about You and all for Your glory. I praise You for the mercy seat miracles You have already done and for the ones You have yet to do. God, You are so good to me! I will tell of Your mercy, Your grace, Your love, and Your goodness for all my days. There is none like You. Praise the Lord!

JimRaleyBooks.com/chp12

A PERSONAL INVITATION
FROM THE AUTHOR

GOD LOVES YOU deeply. His Word is filled with promises that reveal His desire to bring healing, hope, and abundant life to every area of your being—body, mind, and spirit. More than anything, He wants a personal relationship with you through His Son, Jesus Christ.

If you've never invited Jesus into your life, you can do so right now. It's not about religion—it's about a relationship with the One who knows you completely and loves you unconditionally. If you're ready to take that step, simply pray this prayer with a sincere heart:

Lord Jesus, I want to know You as my Savior and Lord. I confess and believe that You are the Son of God and that You died for my sins. I believe You rose from the dead and are alive today. Please for-give me for my sins. I invite You into my heart and my life. Make me new. Help me to walk with You, grow in Your love, and live for You every day. In Jesus' name, amen.

If you just prayed that prayer, you've made the most impor-tant decision of your life. All of heaven rejoices with you, and so do I! You are now a child of God, and your journey with Him has just begun. Please reach out to my publisher at pray4me@charismamedia.com if you accepted Jesus today or if this book has encouraged or impacted your life in any way. We'd love to celebrate with you and send you free materials to help strengthen your faith. We look forward to hearing from you!

NOTES

INTRODUCTION

1. David Guzik, "Numbers 2 – The Camp of Israel," Enduring Word, accessed October 20, 2025, https://enduringword.com/bible-commentary/numbers-2/.
2. Blue Letter Bible, "'ōhel," accessed June 19, 2025, https://www.blueletterbible.org/lexicon/h168/kjv/wlc/0-1/.
3. Blue Letter Bible, "mô'ēḏ," accessed June 19, 2025, https://www.blueletterbible.org/lexicon/h4150/kjv/wlc/0-1/.
4. Blue Letter Bible, "yiśśāśḵār," accessed June 19, 2025, https://www.blueletterbible.org/lexicon/h3485/kjv/wlc/0-1/.
5. Blue Letter Bible, "zᵊḇûlûn," accessed June 19, 2025, https://www.blueletterbible.org/lexicon/h2074/kjv/wlc/0-1/; Blue Letter Bible, "zāḇal," accessed June 19, 2025, https://www.blueletterbible.org/lexicon/h2082/kjv/wlc/0-1/; Blue Letter Bible, "zeḇeḏ," accessed June 19, 2025, https://www.blueletterbible.org/lexicon/h2065/kjv/wlc/0-1/.
6. Blue Letter Bible, "yᵊhûḏâ," accessed June 19, 2025, https://www.blueletterbible.org/lexicon/h3063/kjv/wlc/0-1/.

CHAPTER 1

1. Blue Letter Bible, "šāḇaḥ," accessed June 23, 2025, https://www.blueletterbible.org/lexicon/h7623/kjv/wlc/0-1/.
2. Blue Letter Bible, "hālal," accessed June 23, 2025, https://www.blueletterbible.org/lexicon/h1984/kjv/wlc/0-1/.
3. Blue Letter Bible, "hālal."
4. Blue Letter Bible, "zāmar," accessed June 23, 2025, https://www.blueletterbible.org/lexicon/h2167/kjv/wlc/0-1/.
5. Blue Letter Bible, "tāqa'," accessed June 23, 2025, https://www.blueletterbible.org/lexicon/h8628/kjv/wlc/0-1/.

CHAPTER 2

1. Blue Letter Bible, "pāsaḥ," accessed June 23, 2025, https://www.blueletterbible.org/lexicon/h6452/kjv/wlc/0-1/.

CHAPTER 3

1. Blue Letter Bible, "*ōlâ*," accessed June 23, 2025, https://www.blueletterbible.org/lexicon/h5930/kjv/wlc/0-1/.
2. Blue Letter Bible, "*minḥâ*," accessed June 23, 2025, https://www.blueletterbible.org/lexicon/h4503/kjv/wlc/0-1/.
3. Blue Letter Bible, "*qārbān*," accessed June 23, 2025, https://www.blueletterbible.org/lexicon/h7133/kjv/wlc/0-1/.
4. *Merriam-Webster*, "tribute," accessed June 23, 2025, https://merriam-webster.com/dictionary/tribute.
5. Blue Letter Bible, "*šelem*," accessed June 23, 2025, https://www.blueletterbible.org/lexicon/h8002/kjv/wlc/0-1/.
6. Blue Letter Bible, "*šālam*," accessed June 23, 2025, https://www.blueletterbible.org/lexicon/h7999/kjv/wlc/0-1/.
7. Blue Letter Bible, "*šālôm*," accessed June 23, 2025, https://www.blueletterbible.org/lexicon/h7965/kjv/wlc/0-1/.
8. Blue Letter Bible, "*ḥaṭṭā'āṯ*," accessed June 23, 2025, https://www.blueletterbible.org/lexicon/h2403/kjv/wlc/0-1/.
9. Blue Letter Bible, "*ḥāṭā*," accessed June 23, 2025, https://www.blueletterbible.org/lexicon/h2398/kjv/wlc/0-1/.
10. Blue Letter Bible, "*āšām*," accessed June 23, 2025, https://www.blueletterbible.org/lexicon/h817/kjv/wlc/0-1/.
11. Blue Letter Bible, "*āšam*."
12. *Merriam-Webster*, "trespass," accessed June 23, 2025, https://www.merriam-webster.com/dictionary/trespass.

CHAPTER 5

1. See Anthony Mangun, *Heaven to Earth* (CreateSpace Independent Publishing Platform, 2018).
2. Blue Letter Bible, "*pele'*," accessed June 23, 2025, https://www.blueletterbible.org/lexicon/h6382/kjv/wlc/0-1/.
3. Blue Letter Bible, "*yā'aṣ*," accessed June 23, 2025, https://www.blueletterbible.org/lexicon/h3289/kjv/wlc/0-1/.
4. Blue Letter Bible, "*gibôr*," accessed June 23, 2025, https://www.blueletterbible.org/lexicon/h1368/kjv/wlc/0-1/.
5. Blue Letter Bible, "*geḇer*," accessed June 23, 2025, https://www.blueletterbible.org/lexicon/h1397/kjv/wlc/0-1/.
6. "The Father Absence Crisis in America," National Fatherhood Initiative, accessed June 23, 2025, https://135704.fs1.hubspotusercontent-na1.net/

hubfs/135704/2022%20Strengths%20Based%20Infographics/
NFIFatherAbsenceInfoGraphic.pdf.

7. Blue Letter Bible, "*āḇ*," accessed June 23, 2025, https://www.
   blueletterbible.org/lexicon/h1/kjv/wlc/0-1/.

8. Blue Letter Bible, "*śar*," accessed June 23, 2025, https://www.
   blueletterbible.org/lexicon/h8269/kjv/wlc/0-1/.

9. Blue Letter Bible, "*šālôm*," accessed June 23, 2025, https://
   www.blueletterbible.org/lexicon/h7965/kjv/wlc/0-1/.

CHAPTER 7

1. Blue Letter Bible, "*prothesis*," accessed June 23, 2025, https://
   www.blueletterbible.org/lexicon/g4286/kjv/tr/0-1/.

2. Blue Letter Bible, "*chorēgeō*," accessed June 23, 2025, https://
   www.blueletterbible.org/lexicon/g5524/kjv/tr/0-1/.

3. Blue Letter Bible, "*chorēgeō*."

4. Tractate Menachot 94b, quoted in Mendy Kaminker, "The
   Showbread: The How and Why of the Temple Bread
   Offering," Chabad, accessed June 23, 2025, https://www.
   chabad.org/library/article_cdo/aid/2974301/jewish/The-
   Showbread-The-How-and-Why-of-the-Temple-Bread-
   Offering.htm.

CHAPTER 8

1. Blue Letter Bible, "*ʿāśâ*," accessed June 23, 2025, https://
   www.blueletterbible.org/lexicon/h6213/kjv/wlc/0-1/.

2. Mishnah Tamid 3:8, accessed June 23, 2025, https://www.
   sefaria.org/Mishnah_Tamid.1.1?lang=bi.

CHAPTER 9

1. Mishnah Shekalim 8:5, accessed June 23, 2025, https://www.
   sefaria.org/Mishnah_Shekalim.8.5?lang=bi.

CHAPTER 10

1. Blue Letter Bible, "*mān*," accessed June 23, 2025, https://
   www.blueletterbible.org/lexicon/h4478/kjv/wlc/0-1/.

CHAPTER 11

1. Blue Letter Bible, "*kapōreṯ*," accessed June 23, 2025, https://
   www.blueletterbible.org/lexicon/h3727/kjv/wlc/0-1/.

2. Blue Letter Bible, "*kāp̄ar*," accessed June 23, 2025, https://
   www.blueletterbible.org/lexicon/h3722/kjv/wlc/0-1/.

3. Blue Letter Bible, "*mizrāq*," accessed June 23, 2025, https://www.blueletterbible.org/lexicon/h4219/kjv/wlc/0-1/.

4. Blue Letter Bible, "*zāraq*," accessed June 23, 2025, https://www.blueletterbible.org/lexicon/h2236/kjv/wlc/0-1/.

CHAPTER 12

1. Blue Letter Bible, "*māšaḥ*," accessed June 23, 2025, https://www.blueletterbible.org/lexicon/h4886/kjv/wlc/0-1/.

2. Blue Letter Bible, "*bālal*," accessed June 23, 2025, https://www.blueletterbible.org/lexicon/h1101/kjv/wlc/0-1/.

3. Blue Letter Bible, "*bālal*."

4. Blue Letter Bible, "*bālal*."

You can connect with Apostle Jim Raley in the following ways :

Instagram: @apostleraley
X: @pastorraley
Facebook: ApostleJimRaley
calvaryfl.com